POWER

OF

THE

CHOICE

DENNIS JACKSON

DEDICATION

With the deepest of affections, I dedicate this book to those who have poured into my life and helped shape my perspective to make choices that would bring me to my knees before the throne of the Almighty God. My beautiful wife, Genoa Jackson, the best choice I have made besides Christ, I dedicate this book to you for your love, patience, and godly wisdom. Deacon Walter Jackson, Pastor Rocine Jackson, Bishop James Straughter, Minister Alice Straughter, our parents and mentors in the Lord and life, this book is a product of your labor of love. To my sister, Nora, who, through her gift of books, served as an ignition point in my life that sparked my love for reading and writing. Overseer Margaret Daniels, my second Muh, I dedicate this book to you for your love, obedience, and discernment. To those who read this offering and glean the power of intent and the rewards of making Christ their choice, I dedicate this book to you. Ultimately, I dedicate this book to my Lord and Savior, Jesus Christ, who gave it for His glory. Thank You, Lord, for choosing me to pen this gift to those You love.

CONTENTS

THE CHOICE

Choosing Christ in perpetuity ensures the full power of the benefit is experienced as the full glory of the choice goes to God.

The choice. Just to say the word "choice" does not sound like much or strike any sense of urgency in the mind of the hearer. But I would like to humbly attempt to give this word acknowledgment, body, tangibility, and magnification. In the end, the choice will be established in the minds of all who utter it in the legitimacy of its power and importance. My hope is to cause the reader to recognize the grave significance God awards this simple but poignant word. "How grave?" you ask. So grave that you and I might have access to its power; Jesus came into the world to sacrificially die. We pray that God helps us to perceive the high esteem of this often-used and lightly regarded idiom. And I, too, pray for the reader of these pages to see the same relevant choice and the access of its benefit being offered in every part of their lives through the many decisions they make daily. God is daily desiring that we choose the way of Christ in our everyday encounters. He has set before us this day life and death. His suggestion (*a better word is His instruction*) is for us all to choose life. Let us examine a more practical example of giving visibility and tangibility to a word. I would like to share an experience shared with me early in my life.

My brother, Walter Jackson, was enrolled in a marketing college class in the early 1980s. He was working on an assignment that involved each individual student coming up with a product to market to the class. The marketing prowess concerning the respective product of each individual student was put on display. The grading for this assignment would be predicated on the response received from the class.

As I remember my brother relating this story, he was having difficulty coming up with anything to present. As the day for his presentation was swiftly approaching, he thought in his mind, *I have to get around to it if I am going to pass this class.* Voila! *That is it*, he thought. An around to it was the product he was going to sell his class. His premise was if you were attempting to accomplish anything and hoped for a prosperous or positive conclusion or result, then it was a must you get around to it. Everybody needed one at some time or another. He gave anecdotal scenarios where you would have to get his product "around to it." One scenario may have gone like this. You may be on the road and have a flat tire but need to get to an important meeting at a specific time. To fix the flat tire and get to the meeting expediently, you will need to get around to it. Amidst the laughter and delight of the class, my brother Walter had given the "around to it" acknowledgment, body, tangibility, and magnification.

When Walter related the story to me, I felt an added sense of enlightenment. It is like I had gained a particular perception that everyone did not possess. I saw the around to it in a more significant and meaningful way. We laughed and celebrated his success, and time and life continued. Through all of the years and every one of our triumphs and failures, we went on with life. It is now approximately forty years after I heard that story, but I can still feel that sense of enlightenment every time I hear the words "get around to it." I know the power of those words, the realness and truth they convey, because it has been presented well. This is my hope for "the choice": acknowledgment, body, tangibility, and magnification. During my teen years, my mother presented the choice in another way that made it real to me. The following story depicts that lesson.

A young teenage boy walked through the room of what used to be a coal camp boarding house. The house had five rooms, all in a straight line, and had been transformed to accommodate two adults and nine children. This arrangement made it almost imminent that you would encounter another member of the family when moving through the small edifice. It was summer, and seemingly, without a care in the world, it was the young man's intent to stride by his mother in pursuit of some meaningless, adolescent endeavor. In passing, his mother uttered this question, "What are you going to do?" as she spun around to face him in an abrupt manner, not aggressive, yet demanding his attention and an immediate answer.

Make no mistake about it—she was the boss. Tiny in
stature yet possessed an inner power that might be unassuming
to some, but to this young man, her authority was proven. You
see, these two had history, and he knew she had ruled that house
well, and this was not one of those times you acted as if you did
not hear what was being asked. So he chose his words wisely and
cautiously responded, "What am I going to do about what, Muh?"
She was now looking directly into his eyes; her response was quick
and direct, "What are you going to do when you graduate?" *There
it was, that weird face you made when your science teacher asked
you questions about the homework you did not do the night prior.
You had no inkling of an idea what was being asked or what the
right answer was to their inquiries. You just wanted to give the im-
pression that the answer was in your head somewhere, but for the
life of you, you just could not seem to conjure it up. But his feisty
mother was not deterred by the antics of this amateur trickster.* Before the youngster could utter a single word or attempt to give that
pretentious account of his not-so-well-thought-out plan, his mother
began to rattle off in an almost anticipated and rehearsed fashion...
the choices. "You can go to college, enlist in the military, or get a

job. But one thing is for certain: when you turn eighteen, you are not going to be living here."

The "you are not going to be living here" part was not a choice but her transcending declaration. To be clear, this was not the mother eagle logistically placing thorns in the eaglet's nest, thus causing the adolescent eaglet enough discomfort to exit the nest, take flight, and go it alone. In his mind, this was obviously a burning of the nest and a breaking of the plate. This declaration shook the young man's world of security to its core and jarred his mind into thinking about the choices that had been presented to him.

How was his life going to be affected going forward once the choice was made? That burning question flooded his mind. His whole life had been spent in the hills of West Virginia, and the whole world around his tiny existence was unknown. But the decree had been stated, and the pressure from his mother's declaration was the centermost thought in his mind, and he had to choose. Which one of these choices would he choose, and where would that choice take him? Whatever the choice, life as he knew it was going to change. And it did.

This may come as a surprise to some of the readers of this text and not so much of a surprise to others, but that young man and the author of this book are one and the same...me. My mother, Bishop Rocine Jackson, was the administrator of the choices, and the choice made was to enlist into the United States Air Force. The power of that one choice opened unforeseen opportunities for me. Opportunities for training, education, home ownership, employment, salary increases, business ownership, medical aid, and retirement finances. Making that choice might have involved a little coaxing from my mother but also a little faith that everything was going to work out. I had confidence in the one who presented the choices to me. She had never let me down before, and I saw no reason why she would then. I held her in high regard, and her words...well, her words meant the world to me...and even now... they still do.

Who would have thought the choice to enlist in the air force would come with so many other benefits? Neither when enlisting nor during my time of service were the benefits offered the focus or priority. I had heard sketches about them while serving, but the scant awareness of those benefits failed to hold my attention for any length of time. I was caught up more in the moment of experiencing the world, wrestling with the variances of life, the ups and downs, the attractions, and the distractions. The wrestling with the moment became my everyday endeavor—the ritual that occupied my mind and time. The wrestling with the moment created the disadvantage of not seeing or preparing for the big picture or planning for the lifetime. The classic "I couldn't see the forest for the trees." This inaccurate viewpoint skewed my decision-making capabilities and steered me away from the cognizance of the value of the benefit and ease of access of the privileges that had been afforded me. I lacked perception, causing me to live deficient of the benefits that were already mine. This is the plight of many Christians today. We have made the choice to choose Christ, but we are so busy wrestling with the moments of the world and all it entails that we miss or delay seeing the full benefit of the relationship we have with Christ: the access, the power, the provision, the victory, the blessing, the freedom, the favor, the future. The good thoughts that God has toward us and the expected end that we are reminded of in God's Word is, by our own inordinate perception and actions, what we deem the unexpected.

As Christians, we have to understand where a choice for Christ places us positionally and be acquainted with the advantages provided with that choice. Let us dig a little deeper into our benefits package. Through being the perfect sacrifice for man's transgression, Jesus has wrought an overwhelming victory for us in taking the sting out of death and revoking the graves' victory by conquering death, hell, sin, Satan, flesh, and the world by way of the cross. Every situation or circumstance that is contrary to that victory is covered and defeated as we stand in Him and on His Word. The benefit of Jesus overcoming the world for us and conferring that victory upon us should bring us great joy and calm as we encounter the world and its adversarial forces on a daily basis. In Ephesians 6 the Word tells us that we wrestle not against flesh and blood but against unseen evil forces that are determined to undermine this victory that we have so graciously received. The only way we suffer defeat is if we do not know our benefits package and fail to choose and apply the benefit to each demonic-inspired circumstance or situation. This scripture also implies we focus as soldiers prepared for the attack. Fully equipped, armored, and ready like an army that has the enemy's battle plan and is informed

THE POWER OF THE CHOICE

of the enemy's every impending move. We have the nuclear bomb of God's Word. The Word is the red button to push when you are weary from wrestling. *Why wrestle when we have the bomb*? It is the gracious sacrifice of Christ, His overcoming, His faith, His wisdom, and His Word that facilitate the strength and calm in our spirit to walk in victory, in every instance, by choosing Him continually.

The acknowledgment of and utilization of this truth expels fear and summons rejoicing in what the Lord has accomplished for us. This is more than a fact; He is our truth, peace, and strength drawn from the wells of salvation with joy. We choose to retain the knowledge of God in our hearts and minds, walking in that knowledge, which transfers joy, which manifests through experience the conquering power that accompanies and complements identification with Christ. *"Be of good cheer; I have overcome the world"* (John 16:33, KJV) is His declaration by which Jesus affirms His victory. That declaration, coupled with the assignment of that same victory to us, allows our minds to be free from the cares of this world and grants us room and the wherewithal to focus on what His will is for our lives. The victorious life of Christ in us is the living hope of glory. The victory that overcomes the world is our faith in His victory, our acceptance of the assignment of it to us, and our resting in its assurances. If we believe and accept God's gracious gift, we will be no longer bound by the grip of the mind of the flesh, whereof in the past it showed its mastery over us through the efficacy of its lust. We choose God's life-changing Word, and committing to it, we proclaim its declaration and receive its manifestation. We are free! No more wrestling! Hallelujah!

This is how we realize and experience all the benefits He has for us and walk confidently in those experiences. This is truly the truth that makes us free. The Word says that He will keep us in perfect peace (that is peace with nothing missing and nothing broken in the life that is governed by faith in His Word); those whose minds are stayed, fixed, settled on Him and what He promises. Choose to daily have unshakeable confidence in the One who has promised and His ability to bring those promises to fruition. For the One who has promised is faithful.

It was while I was in the USAF that I also made the most important decision of my life, and that was to give my life to the Lord Jesus Christ. The power and benefits that resulted from that choice alone are immeasurable and innumerable. Receiving Christ is the gift that keeps on giving. My choosing Him and His Word continually is the gift I strive to reciprocally give Him. In return, the benefits of that continual choice flow to me. Choosing Christ in perpetuity ensures the full power of the benefit is experienced as the full glory of the choice goes to God. His praise shall continually be in my mouth.

> Psalm 116:12–14 (NIV):
>
> *"How can I repay the LORD for all His goodness to me?*
> *"I will lift up the cup of salvation and call on the name of the LORD.*
> *"I will fulfill my vows to the LORD in the presence of all His people."*

The psalmist speaks the sentiments of my heart in this passage of Scripture. He is proverbially raising the cup of blessing filled with the knowledge of salvation in a celebratory toast, raising it to give acknowledgment to the goodness of the Lord. He is intently willing a blessing to the Lord, honoring the Lord and giving Him glory for salvation and all the benefits that are packed in it. The caveat is we have to choose God to acquire the cup, then choose to drink, engage, or walk in the knowledge to experience the benefits. A cup of wine has no effect on you as long as it remains in the cup. You have to choose to drink it, consume it for its spirits to take effect. Each sip magnifies the effect of its consumption. Each taste reinvigorates and intensifies the effects of the last sip. *"Oh, taste and see that the Lord is good"* (Psalm 34:8, ESV), and the effect of that goodness endures forever.

God Himself has given humanity the freedom to choose his own destiny. This attribute has made man a self-determinate being. We determine what path of progression or digression we follow, what prosperity or ruin we attain to through and by the choices we make. To serve God or reject God is our choice. This is not a choice of whether we worship God or not but the choice of who we will serve and worship. This choice in itself is significant because worship is man's function; it is what man was created to do. Worship is intrinsically woven into our spiritual DNA. We will always worship something. What or who we worship is a matter of choice; what word we partake of and choose to follow is our preference and ours alone.

We determine the who or what we surrender the throne of our heart to. Just know the power of the choice is to bring your choice's preordained manifestation of consequences...to you.

THE POWER OF THE CHOICE

Just as the choice to join the military brought all the benefits the military life had to offer me. Every benefit is mine; I just have to follow the prerequisites to obtain that for which I already qualify. God desires that we choose Him and follow the prerequisites He has foreordained to realize the blessings He has in store for those who love Him. Choose wisely and follow intently because God has good things in store for you.

First Corinthians 2:9 (KJV):

"But as it is written, Eye hath not seen, nor ear heard, neither have entered into the heart of man, the things [good things] which God hath prepared for them that love him."

Loving God is earnestly choosing Him above all others and having your mind fixed upon Him, obeying His Word, and yielding your body, soul, and spirit to His will every day. This is the choice you have been created for. The choice that matters to God and moves Him to forego judgment and extend to all who choose Him mercy and grace.

YOUR CHOICE WILL
BE CHALLENGED

Mark 1:16–18 (NIV):

"As Jesus walked beside the Sea of Galilee, he saw Simon and

his brother Andrew casting a net into the lake, for they were

fishermen. 'Come, follow me,' Jesus said, 'and I will send you out

to fish for people.' At once they left their nets and followed him."

Peter was one of the first disciples chosen and called by
Jesus. You would think being called by Jesus in the days of His
flesh would preclude you from facing any danger of failing and
quash every challenge to your state and standing. It would also

stand to earthly reason your answering His call and following Him, would preclude you from facing any challenger or would-be challenge mounted that would attempt a stand against the faith you had in Christ. There must be some guarantee of your constant victory over sin, self, and Satan without challenge. Right? Just ask Peter. He has experience in this area and would surely be able to provide an answer that can give insight and direction. His dealings with his measure of inward challenges have been well documented. Not only would Peter's choices be challenged, but also Jesus' choice of Peter was being challenged also.

Peter has been labeled by some as the presumptuous disciple. This simply means Peter thought more of himself than he should and acted out of that forward thought more often than he should have. Often you find Peter, more than the other disciples, being chided by Jesus for statements and moves made according to his own reasoning, without consideration for what the heart of the Lord desired. This behavior would exemplify confidence in flesh and pride in self, demonstrating disbelief in the power of Jesus Christ to accomplish those things that were deemed difficult or uncomfortable. This is the challenge. Do we believe God or trust in our own way, our own strength, and our own self?

For approximately three and a half years, Peter walked with Christ as one of the core members, which consisted of three disciples who were considered His inner circle. Peter was allowed to be a part of, witness, and hear things the other disciples were not privy to. For three and a half years, Peter had heard the sermons, witnessed the transfiguration, seen the miracles, and witnessed the expansion of the ministry of which Jesus was the central figure. Peter had himself witnessed the power of God working in his own person as he went out in the authority of Jesus with the seventy, casting out demons and carrying the Word of God when sent out by Jesus to minister to every town and place. He was the disciple who was summoned by Jesus in the midst of a storm and allowed to walk on water. The very same disciple who was given the revelation from the Father of who Christ was when no one else could answer Jesus' inquiry. It was to Peter Jesus gave the keys of the kingdom of heaven that would unlock faith and obedience and bind fear and unbelief at Pentecost, unlocking mystery of salvation to the upper room Christians. In all of these triumphs, challenge was also ever-present. Your choice for Christ and for the truth of

THE POWER OF THE CHOICE

His Word will be challenged every day. As long as you are on this earth, there will be relentless attacks on your faith by the enemy of your soul.

While attending the Last Supper, Jesus said these words to Peter.

Luke 22:31–32 (KJV):

And the Lord said, Simon, Simon, behold, Satan hath desired to have you, that he may sift you as wheat:

But I have prayed for thee, that thy faith fail not: and when thou art converted, strengthen thy brethren.

Here Jesus was preparing to die. He was telling His disciples of the perils that were prophesied of Him and soon to be fulfilled. Even then they were thinking about themselves and jockeying for a heavenly position. Jesus was preparing them for His upcoming trial and eventual death, burial, and resurrection. He knew they would disperse, so He planted the aforementioned word in His presumptuous disciple Peter. *After you have been challenged, after your failure to overcome that challenge, after you have betrayed Me, after you have seen yourself, repented, and are restored to right thinking, strengthen your brethren.* In Peter's normal naïve and presumptuous fashion, he stated his loyalty and how far he would go in defense of Jesus. Of course, before the cock crowed, Peter had betrayed, denied, and abandoned Christ. His choice for Christ had been challenged, and he failed to stand in truth.

My friend, do not be naïve and think that God is the only entity wooing you for control of your life through the surrendered reins of your heart. You do have a very present enemy that is contending for your choice and the mastery of your decision-making faculties: your mind, your will, and your emotions. Your adversary is Satan. His desire is to confuse you concerning your purpose, setting his words on the throne of your heart, possessing your reins, and navigating you toward destruction. His desire and aim, unlike God's, are far from good. The enemy's aim is to challenge your faith; distort your intent, steering you away from the presence of your Savior; and drive you to ruin. His desire is to entangle your mind in the deception of the lust of the flesh, the lust of the eye, and the pride of life, grounding you in that deception so deep that you reject any semblance of truth or faith. Satisfying the insatiable appetite of self is the mind and will of the flesh. Some go down that road guilt-ridden, many fearful, and some are confidently, even happily, deceived, preferring the pleasures of sin that last only for a season, embracing the inevitable death.

This is the very reason we have so many broken and wayward souls that feel they lack the ability to pull themselves out of the dilemma in which they have been entrapped. This addiction to self is real, and there is one who promotes every indulgence of its desire. Friend, Satan is that enemy of our souls that will feed you the poison pill of the knowledge of evil, knowing you will not be able to resist it without choosing Christ. It is of the utmost importance we understand we are at war, under attack, and the treasure of our soul is in jeopardy of death by a wrong choice. But be assured that God is offering the world life-giving truth in Jesus Christ, by which we are able to resist the suggestions of the devil and urgings of the flesh and overcome evil with good. All who choose to reject the life-giving truth in Jesus and believe the devil's lie will meet a disastrous end.

In his quest to shipwreck man and disallow God His glory, Satan has bombarded man with so many deceptive words and thoughts. Amplifying the desires of the flesh, he is attempting to place a fraudulent word securely in the hearts of man. Words that would be followed by acts of worship directed to please an undeserving idol called self. This was the scenario that played out in the garden of Eden with our first parents, Adam and Eve. Satan hoped to steal God's worship and secure that seat in the human heart, a throne that was designed and reserved for God and His Word alone. His mind was set on stealing, killing, and destroying God's man. His desire was to challenge the authority of God in man and frustrate man's purpose—that purpose being making God and His Word man's priority, his first choice, his aim and intent. It was the introduction of a demonic word that would cause Adam and Eve to forsake the Word of God that had been delivered to them. Eve was deceived into receiving that seed of doubt. Through deceit she received the deceitful word that would poison her thinking and distort how she saw God. Adam chose that same transgressing word and committed the treasonous act of dethroning his Creator, the True and Living God, from the throne of his heart, replacing the Word of God with the duplicitous word of a supplanter, the deceiver, that old serpent Satan. Adam displaced the Word that was responsible for his connection to God and the glory that clothed him. That day, Adam was separated from God and experienced spiritual death. The consequence of a wrong choice. Did we get that? The placement of God's Word in your heart is vital to a successful life in Christ. This is a willful act that you do. David said it best in Psalm 119:11 (KJV), "*Thy word have I hid in [the center of the throne of] mine heart that I might not sin against thee.*" Some translations use the word "treasured" in place of "hid" to infer preference and value.

Because Adam did not stand against the challenge and choose God because he did not value or prefer the word that was placed in his heart over self and all else, the glory that had clothed him and his companion day and night left him. This naked and sinful state Adam found himself in is the inheritance that we received from Adam. We are born into the world as spiritual beings separated from God because of sin, covered in naked flesh, spiritually dead. Outside of our natural environment (which is the presence of God), Adam's and our death are imminent. Adam's choice left him separated from God, gripped by fear, instead of being clothed with glory and walking in confident love and power.

Adam was now ill-equipped to fend off the plethora of ills that the world would bring to eventually administrate his physical death. This was not God's plan A for man. What Adam was experiencing now was the power of the wrong choice. The right choice, the godly choice, had been challenged and rejected.

Since that incident, Satan has used this tactic many times over to shipwreck God's will for His man and to denigrate man to a fraction of what he can be and experience. So many idol gods have been created to pretentiously massage the psyche and emotions of man, satisfying the flesh for a season yet still leaving the man either spiritually crippled or spiritually dead. So many people unsuspectingly have bought into the devil's lies to the worshipping of many idol gods.

Polytheism, the pluralistic worshipping of many gods, is the result of those lies and has, for many, become the norm in much of the world. The nominal Christian has scoffed and ridiculed this type of religion for many years. When in fact, many a Christian's heart throne has been the proverbial hot seat for the idol god of their choice to occupy. Your idol god is that thing or thought preferred before God and allowed to operate from your heart, which is His place of authority. This takes place when Christ is politely asked to step down from His place of authority while we indulge in what we have been gifted and entertain what we have been baited by: our besetting sin.

Tragic but true.

For Satan, to get you to obey his word for a while could deter, distract, or dismantle your assignment or prevent you from fulfilling your God-given purpose momentarily. What are the consequences of that? What if the person who spoke the word into your life was deterred, distracted, or momentarily dismantled from their purpose, and the word you needed to cause you to say yes to the Lord was not delivered? What if the same thing happens to a million people daily? Instead of a life-giving word, a deceptive word is placed in their heart. By that deceptive word, Satan hopes to deter and disconnect them from the truth that makes them free. This has been one of his most effective tools by which he attempts to weaken the church and cause them to be inconsistent in obeying the truth. Sometimes on and sometimes off, unstable in our walks, unstable in our ways. Not being steadfast and unmovable, not being single-eyed, not letting our yeas be yea and our nays be nay.

The Bible calls this being double-minded. The man who has this title need not think he can ask God for anything and see it come to pass. Are we seeing it yet?

If it seems that things are not working in your life, this simplistic revelation should be eye-opening to you. I have to say that it is to me. You have asked God for things, and it seems as if you cannot get an answer; nothing seems to work out for you. This is the time to take an introspective look at your relationship with the God of heaven and earth and see how your life is aligning with His Word. *Is God's Word at the center of my being? Is the truth of God's Word the focus and aim of my life? Is my intent to please God only, and are my decisions in life being directed and powered by the inexhaustible and perfect truths the Word provides?* If you discover that this is not your reality, the Lord has not left you without remedy. You will find out that all is not lost. Repent and get realigned with the truth. Make your aim true. Our mindset can be tweaked to please God through repentance and placing the transformative Word of God in its purposed place. Aim to center the Word of God in your heart and do it. This is what it means to have Christ, who is the Word, in the center of your heart. Let God know He is preferred and valued in your life. We must consider the One who sacrificed it all so that we might have the opportunity to approach God and have a fruitful relationship with Him. Consider Him, who endured the contradiction of sinners against Himself by keeping the joy of seeing you enter into the kingdom of God in His view. He became obedient to death to secure our overwhelming victory, fulfilling His Father's joy. Faith in the heart-centered Word of God and relying on what He has accomplished allows us to walk in His sweatless victory. We become overcomers because He overcame. We are more than conquerors. Because He has gifted us His victory of conquering anything that would oppose God's acceptance of us. My friend, please understand that warfare isn't easy when you do not follow God's chosen battle plan. To guard our hearts and resist the influences of the evil one is our daily battle through our choices. This can only be successful if we continue to cultivate our relationship with the Lord Jesus Christ by choosing His Word in every presented situation.

My father, Deacon Walter Jackson, had a saying that has been a staple in my life when dealing with relationships. He would say, "It is a poor wind that doesn't blow both ways." The meaning of this simple statement is profound in its accuracy when defining what constitutes a true relationship.

The statement finds great usefulness in its application in maintaining or building a relationship. Without the contributions of both parties (thus both ways) involved in a relationship (the wind), a good and true relationship does not exist (poor wind or poor relationship). It is upon this premise that we conclude that this is what God desires: a good and true relationship with His people. A reciprocal response to Him choosing us would be for us to choose Him. Choice for choice, love for love, respect for respect, sacrifice for sacrifice.

God has made us for fellowship, communion, and worship. God's contribution is evident. With each morning's dawn, God supplies us with a breath of life, activity of our limbs, new mercies, graces, and opportunities to choose and experience the advantages of His favor and wisdom, which He graciously supplies. It is through His wisdom we make decisions that please and glorify Him and His purpose. Those same decisions bring God glory and bring blessings into our lives. He has truly shown that He is married to and loves his man Adam, the backslider. So much so that he sent His Son to die for his redemption. He has longed for the day to be reunited with His creation and enjoy the reciprocal pleasures of their union in worship—those days when they walked in agreement through the garden in fellowship, Adam being clothed with the same majestic glory that the God of heaven was adorned with. God satisfying the need and purpose of man to worship the True God, and man experiencing the fullness of salvation by it. Man, in turn, satisfies the will of the Most High God: that being to freely love the Lord God with all his heart and put no other god before Him. God is seeking that kind of relationship.

John 4:23–24 (KJV):

> *"But the hour cometh, and now is, when the true worshippers shall worship the Father in spirit and in truth: for the Father seeketh such to worship him.*
>
> *"God is a Spirit: and they that worship him must worship him in spirit and in truth."*

We can see how Jehovah God sought that relationship with the children of Israel. God had wrenched the children of Israel from the bonds of Egyptian slavery and created a miraculous path through the Red Sea to bring them deliverance from the clutches of the Egyptian army. God then used the same Red Sea to bring judgment to a malicious Pharaoh and his army, which subsequently drowned while in pursuit of the newly-freed and thought-vulnerable Israelites. For forty years they wandered in the wilderness. God miraculously sustained them; the very clothes on their backs and shoes on their feet did not encounter normal wear. They drank sweet water from a rock and feasted on manna from on high. They received the law contained in the Ten Commandments from the finger of God. They were taught the intricacies of worship in the wilderness tabernacle and learned the fear of the Lord. Moses died before entering the promised land, but God did not leave them without a chosen and capable successor to shepherd them into their possession. Joshua had led the Israelites across a divinely divided Jordan River and was led by the commander of the Lord's army in their conquest of displacing the heathenistic inhabitants of the promised land. Conquest after conquest, battle after battle, was accompanied by victory after victory. God was the head of the spear and was with them at the front of the battle. God was making good on His promise to Abraham, Isaac, and Jacob.

THE POWER OF THE CHOICE

The children of Israel have now occupied the promised land for approximately twenty-five years. The Lord has shown them His power, guidance, favor, mercy, grace, truth, protection, provision, faithfulness, and righteousness for approximately sixty-five years since their release from bondage. Now God is requiring a commitment from the people He has chosen and loved. It is not enough for us to receive the treasures of God's love without a reciprocal response. That response is making God our choice and serving the God who has so graciously supplied us with His goodness. That response is making God and His Word the center of our lives, the intent of our hearts. That response is our worship.

Joshua has gathered Israel to Shechem to deliver this message from the El Shaddai and to make a solemn declaration that will cause all Israel to take an introspective look at where they have placed God in their lives. It is here their champion speaks.

Joshua 24:14–15 (ESV):

Now therefore fear the Lord and serve him in sincerity and in faithfulness. Put away the gods that your fathers served beyond the River and in Egypt and serve the Lord. And if it is evil in your eyes to serve the Lord, choose

34

this day whom you will serve, whether the gods your fathers served in the region beyond the River, or the gods of the Amorites in whose land you dwell. But as for me and my house, we will serve the Lord.

The choice was set before them of who they would serve, not *if* they would serve. The truth is that man is going to serve; he is going to worship a god, whether he be true or idol, because worship is the fabric that we produce. We clothe God in honor, majesty, worship, and praise. We glorify Him (*allow God's opinion, His will, to be exercised in our lives*). That is the nature of who we are and what we were created to do. Just like the nature of an apple tree is to produce apples. What you are going to use those apples for is of no consequence to the tree. It just keeps cranking out apples. The tree does not have a choice. Worship is the product we produce. Joshua understood God's desire. The apple, product, service, and worship that he produced, he chose to give to God for His purpose.

God is asking His children to use their God-given faculty, which makes mankind a self-determined being, to choose Him, to love Him, to place God's Word in their heart, and produce worship

THE POWER OF THE CHOICE

for Him and Him only. This is what we were designed to do. He is asking us to make the right choice. The same choice He made while being tempted by the devil in the wilderness.

Luke 4:5–8 (AMP):

Then he led Jesus up [to a high mountain] and displayed before Him all the kingdoms of the inhabited earth [and their magnificence] in the twinkling of an eye.
And the devil said to Him, "I will give You all this realm and its glory [its power, its renown]; because it has been handed over to me, and I give it to whomever I wish. Therefore if You worship before me, it will all be Yours."
Jesus replied to him, "It is written and forever remains written, 'YOU SHALL WORSHIP THE LORD YOUR GOD AND SERVE ONLY HIM.'"

With every temptation or adversarial encounter, Jesus constantly chose the Father and worshipped Him. He is making this appeal to the whole world. Choose Him! Our gift to God for His grace toward us is the surrendering of our will, our choice, our opinion, our way, and our life to God's will and desire. To worship Christ is our purpose, our aim, and our goal.

Deuteronomy 30:14, 19–20 (KJV):

But the word is very nigh unto thee, in thy mouth, and in thy heart, that thou mayest do it.

I call heaven and earth to record this day against you, that I have set before you life and death, blessing and cursing: therefore, choose life, that both thou and thy seed may live:

That thou mayest love the Lord thy God, and that thou mayest obey his voice, and that thou mayest cleave unto him: for he is thy life, and the length of thy days: that thou mayest dwell in the land which the Lord sware unto thy fathers, to Abraham, to Isaac, and to Jacob, to give them.

The power of the choice has eternal foundations.

Psalm 119:89 (KJV),

"Forever Oh Lord thy word is settled in heaven."

Those foundations produce eternal ramifications.

John 5:24 (AMP):

I assure you and most solemnly say to you, the person who hears My word [the one who heeds My message], and

THE POWER OF THE CHOICE

believes and trusts in Him who sent Me, has (possesses now) eternal life [that is, eternal life actually begins--the believer is transformed], and does not come into judgment and condemnation, but has passed [over] from death into life.

He who has an ear let him hear. The sum of our existence has been encapsulated by the Word. Every encounter has been considered and covered. The game is afoot, and the choice is yours. He has shown that His thoughts are continually good toward us through His goodness and merciful kindness we experience daily. God's character is proven throughout the ages, and His goodness and loving-kindness are openly accessible to all those who will taste and see that the Lord is good, and His mercy is extended and endures forever to those who choose Him. It is now time for us to take responsibility and make what we have with God a wind that blows both ways, a true relationship that brings a coexisting joy for you and God, as it was in the beginning. Make a conscious decision today to surrender your choice and life to Christ and live His.

Stand against the challenges of the devil. Resist him, and he will flee from you. His wiles are cunning and deceitful, but God has not left us ignorant of his tactics. Though the challenge to your faith is real, we have a God who says many are the affliction of those who trust in Him, but He will deliver, free, and rescue you from them all. Just stand firm and do not relent. Have faith in His ability to demonstrate and secure salvation for you.

IN PURSUIT OF VIRTUE

There is no power without pursuit.

To start this chapter without a working definition of the word "virtue," I think, would be remiss. When we define "virtue" in our own minds, I believe many of us land on the side of moral correctness or goodness. But the Greeks thought differently about this word and associated it with function. The power of virtue is at the heart of this writing and has everything to do with our connection with God through and by His Word. Let us explore.

Virtue:

The Greek word for virtue is "ARETE." For the Greeks, the notion of virtue is tied to the notion of function (ER-GON). The virtues of something are what enable it to perform excellently its proper function. Virtue (or arete) extends beyond the realm of morality; it concerns the excellent performance of any function.

Haslanger 2017

The quest for truth should be the epic journey of each individual's life, and the discovery of truth should be the greatest reward and joy. Jesus is the truth. Not knowing the truth sets one up for a host of missteps and failures. Knowing the truth creates a pathway to realized accomplishments and indisputable freedom. Continuing to pursue and commune with the knowledge of truth makes those accomplishments and freedom your realized salvation and blessing.

THE POWER OF THE CHOICE

It is a truth that God created the world to reflect His nature and glory. The God we serve is love, and He is glorified through and by the deliberate obedience, intentional worship, and willful adoration of His creation. It is also a truth that God, being without fault, is perfect light. In Him is no shadow of turning, and there is no darkness in Him at all. He is infallible. He is, in the greater sense of the word...perfect. He speaks, and whatever He says happens, comes to be, comes to fruition. His power works perfectly. He is the Great I Am. At the voice of His Word, creation responds. Each element, moving in harmonic waves, conducted by His will, finds its appointed place, synchronizing like notes performed by a symphonic orchestra. Moving to create beautiful music collectively the notes render an orchestral arrangement that delights the soul. God smiles and says, "It is good" for His purpose to His glory. His Word operates perfectly, and everything that God created was good and blessed, having the distinct capacity to be good. God's Word, filled with virtue, made it so. All of creation functioned excellently. Within the boundary of God's virtue, the sun, moon, and stars followed their courses and ruled in their respective places, functioning perfectly. Because the Creator was at the helm, His Word working to perform, everything worked as it should. It was good because God's will was being orchestrated through them by their obedience to the Word. He had given them their assignment to rule, and if they remained in their place, in the truth, doing what God had commanded them to do, their reign would continue in perfection.

God spoke words. Creative words with the power to produce the expression of images He voiced. From the smallest molecule to the largest of oceans, throughout the expanse of space, all operated under His command. *"Be ye holy, for I am holy"* (Leviticus 11:44, KJV) is what God has spoken in our lives. Is it any wonder that the desire of God's heart is that we mimic His perfection, His righteousness, and His holiness through obedience to His Word? His Word will perform and replicate God's will in all those who submit to it to all who have an intentional relationship with it. God is His Word, and His Word is Him. After all, we are His children and are made in His image and likeness. Adam had a word placed in his life, and He was perfect—his functionality flawless. He was divinely equipped to operate excellently as long as he allowed God's Word to continually occupy the seat of authority within his heart. He was moving on God's command, but there was another voice he should not follow. Adam was a sheep of the Lord's pasture. This Adam was and did all that was required of him as he enjoyed the fruits of perfection, which are obtained through and by adherence to God's Word. Life, health, strength, healing, protection, provision, love, joy, power, peace, nothing missing and nothing broken, long-suffering, goodness, gentleness, faith, temperance, wisdom, and all good things were his through keeping God as the center of his life. All this Adam possessed and lived perfectly before God until he did not. Adam went after and chose another word and was separated from God. "Self-elected" to assign the seat of the throne of man's heart to the word of a devil-possessed serpent. And there, flesh began its carnal rule. This is the fallen state that defines all men who do not have our Lord and Savior at the head of their lives. Broken. Only a fraction of what God created us to be. Our spirit still longs to be what the mind of God had purposed, but it is buried inside a derivative of the dust we walk on, a grave called flesh. The spirit man that was created in the image of God has now been assigned to the depths of the human heart and separated from God until the sentence he so justly deserved has been fully executed. That sentence was death.

So how do we get back into fellowship with God and rise in newness of life, reclaiming what Adam lost, allowing His power to work in us as He has purposed? Only with the seating of the rightful King on the throne prepared only for Him and our awareness of His essential and sovereign reign can this blessed communion be accomplished in us. Only then can God's virtue be released to accomplish salvation in and through us. Every aspect of our lives, every situation we face, every circumstance we encounter, we must make Jesus Lord over it. It is to Him we must direct our gaze and focus earnestly on His Word for our living. God's Word must be above all, through all, and in you all. After hearing the Word, we embrace it and pursue God. As we come into His presence, His virtue that brings all things under His order pursues the faith-gripped word and makes all things function according to what He has spoken. The throne of our heart must be relinquished to the whims of His will. We must pursue and submit to the King of kings and Lord of lords as His virtue pursues His words—the power of God that makes all things operate exceptionally to the extent of their designed purpose.

THE POWER OF THE CHOICE

This concept is illustrated very well in Mark 4:25–34. In the story of the woman with the issue of blood. But first, there are a few things that we must consider when pondering this passage of Scripture. The first is the circumstance we find this woman in. For twelve long years, she had a continual bleeding from her body, an infirmity. Her body was not operating properly. In fact, her problem was deeper than physical. She had a malfunction in her heart that affected her body, soul, and spirit. There was a thought that occupied her heart. A word that was wreaking havoc in her life. That thought occupied the center of her being and dominated her thoughts. Her issue was at odds with the truth of the purpose man was designed for. This woman had an issue that only the correct alignment with the Word of God could correct.

Because of her illness, she suffered many things at the hands of physicians. The Bible does not detail all she suffered, but we can only imagine a primitive solution to an ailment like this one. According to the history of medicine, a primitive treatment could involve some bizarre and painful antidotes that would be considered cruel and extreme by present-day standards and practices, often ending in failure. Sometimes loss of life was the outcome.

This woman, through constantly seeking out medical attention, had not only been literally stripped of her wealth but her dignity as well. Year after year, treatment after failed treatment, disappointment after disappointment, her situation worsened. The psychological weight was increased by the societal response to her condition. According to the law, she was to be isolated, not allowed to go to her place of worship. She was to be shunned, ostracized, and labeled unclean. If she came in physical contact with anyone in her daily commuting, they, too, were to be considered unclean. They would have to submit to a ceremonial purification prerequisite to be cleansed of this unclean status spawned from contact with this cursed woman. She was robbed of her purpose, living a dismal, diminished, and devastated life, and her self-worth and identity had been stripped away by this lingering illness. Her former social status and standing had been renounced, and now she was considered a stain on society. Her issue was draining her. To touch Jesus, in everyone else's mind, would have been an offense of the highest degree and would have made Him unclean. But it was this Jesus that possessed the very thing that she needed, and without knowing it, she had been equipped with the very thing to obtain it.

THE POWER OF THE CHOICE

Knowledge of God's power and grace had put her faith in pursuit of virtue. With a tenacious hunger for the Word heard and now hidden in her heart, she pressed through the crowd that had congregated around and followed Jesus. The crowd pressed Him on every side, but she pressed through the crowd because her situation was dire. She pressed because God's Word had found a place of deposit in her heart, a place of harbor in her innermost being, where she allowed God's Word to be anchored and her faith to be activated. That Word sought its manifestation. The Word and her faith would combine to propel her into belief. She pressed into Jesus, believing she could not possess the performance of power without pursuit.

"For she said within herself, If I may but touch his garment, I shall be whole" (Matthew 9:21, KJV).

This was the truth that was in the depths of her heart, her mantra in the moment. Coupled with the knowledge and faith that Jesus was a healer, one sent from God, the Messiah. His fame had gone out, and the word on the street was this man was the Son of God. Her belief in what she had heard and who He was and what He could do in her life overcame her fear, the opinion of others, and even her own self-doubt and moved her into declaration and belief. The word was out, so she pressed through the crowd and reached in.

The arm of the flesh had failed her so many times. She had come to the end of her wits, the end of her own thinking on how to escape this bondage and torment she was experiencing. She had come to the end of relying on man and his limited knowledge of how God's creation works and what to do when it is broken. She had tried everything, and everything had failed her. She was cornered by desperation; one choice was all she could see. Try Jesus the Living Word, a surer Word, a surer way.

For twelve years, unsure words, posing as a remedy, had crept into her heart, promising hope, calling for her action, and delivering disappointment. It was like chasing the wind and catching it to no avail. Still unclean. Try this medicine or this tonic. Still unclean. Perhaps there were a series of surgeries that this desperate soul was subjected to or a string of treatments that did more harm than good. Still unclean. The evil suggestion that this was her state of affairs, her lot in life, and the longevity of the condition presented the idea it was almost certain that she would die this way. Her reality was to stay out of sight, out from under the radar, disconnected from human touch.

This is the result of the Word now defining her existence. A resounding…unclean.

Everywhere she grappled for another word, for a remedy… to no avail. She was like the rest of unregenerated men, searching for a truth to believe in, a word that would free them from the word that had them bound, that bondage-producing word…"sinner." What is the word in your life that has you bound and reaching for remedies and solutions? Is it divorce, cancer, sickness, disease, lack, thief, fornicator, adulterer, liar, unworthy, unrighteous, self-absorbed, unaware…? She needed the truth of God's Word to be deposited into her life to change the condition in which she was trapped. She had been looking for her solution in all the wrong places, but now the truth would be passing by. The Word was near to her, and she had the audacity to speak it in faith and move to it. The very thing that she had been seeking was now exposed to her longing, within her reach, pending her touch. Jesus, the Living Word, who brings salvation to those who will let Him in. This is the same situation that is playing out today as you sit and read these words that have been divinely placed in your view. The truth is here. Jesus is here right now to oppose the word that has placed you in bondage and release a word into your life that will execute your exoneration. Be whole by letting your faith in the Lord Jesus Christ and His Word find its designed place in your heart. The correctly-placed word will compel you to press into His presence where there is fulness of joy, wholeness, and power to restore and build you into the man or woman of God you were created to be. Press in and make contact.

How did she hear about this Jesus and the healing virtue that accompanied Him? Perchance, someone, even not directly, related that Jesus the healer was in town. She may have overheard of the miracles that had been wrought by His hand. Perhaps she had heard of His statements to others after a notable miracle, *"According to your faith be it unto you"* (Matthew 9:29, KJV). Someone had expressed a word of truth, and she latched onto it, depositing it into her heart and rehearsing it in her mind; she uttered it with her mouth. Most importantly, she mixed that word with faith and began to walk through obstacles that would have otherwise deterred her. When she was devoid of the power of the freedom-giving truth, the boldness to step up and press in did not exist. She would have been halted from a straight walk and confined to an isolated and solitary place by the reigning word that had been sitting on the throne of her heart for twelve long years. That same word that had driven her to ruin…"unclean."

No one would touch her. She lived in fear of physical contact lest she contaminated others and became the object of ridicule, rebuke, and judgment. The cost of a touch would be incurring the social, religious, and political fallout of a society she had previously been a prominent part of but now is contrary to and estranged from. Yet she longed for touch, for connection, for communication, but the word unclean prevents it. That word…"unclean" forbade it. For twelve years the demonic spirit called unclean reigned and produced the pain and trauma this woman endured.

Perhaps she perceived the possibilities that were in this man called Jesus. Possibly the thought arose in her mind, *This is the day I receive my healing; I will draw a line in the sand today and tell this demon, "No more, not today, because God's Word has given me a foundation, a footing, a hope, an expected end. You can go no further, not this time." I will declare the Word of the Lord; I will declare what I believe and progress toward it, and the*

God of heaven will lift up a standard against your attacks. If I can just touch the hem of His garment. She moved through the crowd with persuaded purpose, a faith-driven tenacity that sought an anticipated end. She had never experienced the drive of a correctly heart-placed truth before. Finally, she had a powerful-established truth seated in her heart; she could cling to it, follow it, and rest in it. She dwelt on that thought; she had one mind, and that mind was to be in close proximity to Jesus. Intent upon reaching Him, her heart's deep calling, reaching for His deep response. The Word had brought her to the realization that Jesus was the only One who had the abundant-inexhaustible supply that could meet her deep and desperate need. She excluded all other outcomes and allowed herself one expectation, and that was to be healed of this unmerciful infirmity that had plagued her these twelve years. *If I can just touch the hem of His garment.* This was an act propelled by faith she must need to perform. This is the action that connects her faith to her manifestation. Just as Abraham's obedient step connected his faith with the promises of God. There was confidence in her heart's declaration as she moved with conviction toward her mark, walking in faith toward what she had heard was the evidence of her expectation. She was pushed by divine persuasion, so she pressed, "If I can only…" What she heard was the evidence not seen yet, but her hope had substance. She could look around and see what Jesus had done for others. She knew in her heart that if He could fulfill the hopes, dreams, and needs of others through His Word, her miracle was a realization awaiting her move. This was the moment for movement into manifestation. *If I can just touch the hem…contact.*

I can imagine some of the people who were crowded around Jesus. Many might have known her; some did not, and some may have only known of her condition but not known her issue. The Word of God went to the root of the matter, corrected her perception, and took care of her issue before she got to Jesus. The virtue, the power that resided inside the body of Jesus, took care of her condition. If the body of Christ is going to see the move of God like seen in biblical times, we must have a paradigm shift; we must lay hold of this concept. Healing takes place in the Word. Provision takes place in the Word. Peace takes place in the Word. Power takes place in the Word. God's Word is what we must hide in our heart, anchor it there, make room for it, believe in it, declare it, and then it will accomplish whatever we say in faith. We must pursue the Word first and give it its proper place before virtue can be released. There can be no power without pursuit. The Word-filled heart will order your steps of faith to the proper positioning, at the throne of grace, humbly at the feet of Jesus to receive virtue for manifestation. The Word works; it just requires a proper place to work from. Our hearts will do. From the depths of our hearts, we believe it, and our mouths will declare it. God's virtue will make God's promises, gifts, anointings, and callings function in excellence in us, toward us, through us, and for us, throughout the ages.

As we seek our Lord and Savior in our daily pursuits, let us have an ear to hear what thus says the Lord when the enemy attempts to steal our joy, kill our dreams, and destroy our destiny.

God is telling us now to forsake the tendency to depend on anything but Him. When it looks like you are losing the fight, remember to let your mind pursue Jesus, the Living Word, within whom the virtuous power that makes all thing function excellently resides. Seek His face and focus on the Word of God and the results that He Himself promises. As He told David when his camp had been attacked and all his people and goods had been stolen:

pursue. Do not pursue the enemy or the stuff that was stolen but pursue God's Word, and the results promised will follow. There will be no power that makes your situation look like what God has spoken without proper placement of God's Word and pursuit. Follow the steps the Word provides. Let your hearing the Word produce the God kind of faith that works by love and replaces fear. With intent, earnestly press into the presence of the Lord, expectantly looking for Him only. It is then that His presence relinquishes the virtue that manifests wholeness. Whatever the Word articulates, virtue maintains at its highest functioning level and generates peace (nothing missing and nothing broken) in the lives of those who, at that moment, want nothing more than the presence of God. This God does with pleasure, satisfying the longings of your soul through the life-changing power of the Great God and our Savior, Jesus Christ. Selah.

EVERYTHING STARTS
WITH A WORD

John 1:1 (KJV), *"In the beginning was the Word and the Word was with God and the Word was God."*

The sky is dark with clouds laden with rain. The wind swirling, thunder bellowing, lightning striking, and the waves are now unrelenting; one wave crashing after the other. Before journeying out to sea, maybe someone should have checked the weather forecast and given these guys a heads-up on the situation they were about to get into. Now here we are…in the middle of a storm.

THE POWER OF THE CHOICE

It is within the scenario of a storm that we find the disciple Peter. He and his contemporaries are caught up in the midst of the fury of the sea. Along with his fellows, fear and faithlessness have gripped the presumptuous disciple. It is in the midst of this storm that Peter is presented choices that have him standing on the cusp of mediocrity or greatness. With one foot planted on the floor of the boat and the other on top of the starboard side, he anticipates a step. But wait, before we get too far into this story, let us back up a bit, tighten the lens, and look a little closer, for there is a truth to be gleaned here.

We are in the middle of the deep, crossing the Sea of Galilee, when a storm arises. Peter and eleven of his fellow disciples are terrified by the sight of what is coming toward them, an image eerily approaching; it seems to be moving, walking on the water's surface and amidst the storm. Wind and rain beating on their faces, thunder rolling one boom after the other, lightning striking lighting up the unnerving sky, waves still crashing all around them, thrashing the boat to and fro. The boat's passengers share one emotion. That emotion is fear.

The disciples, those chosen few that had been with Jesus,

all submit to their fears and cower at the approaching specter. Just days before, you would imagine their faith had been fed and lifted when Jesus miraculously fed the five thousand with just two fish and five loaves of bread. You would think they would still be on a spiritual high and realize an increase of faith, a particular empowerment from witnessing and being a part of such a notable miracle. Now, in the middle of the Sea of Galilee, that same seedling faith is being challenged by a storm.

They see what they assume is an apparition, but it is Jesus, the Living Word approaching them, treading above what would be to some a watery grave. Peter realizes that it is Jesus, and for some reason, his focus seems to change from the storm to just Jesus. His aim is now to get to Jesus in spite of the storm. It is as if nothing else matters but Jesus at this point. In that moment Peter chooses Jesus as his focus. This decision gives rise to that faith and ignites the desire to be like Him and with Him where He is. For a moment, we get a glimpse of the faith that had been witnessed and strengthened days before while distributing the miraculous meal to the five thousand. With each fraction of bread broken off and distributed, another fraction was generated and awaited distribution. Peter must have thought, *This is that same Jesus. The One who calls things that be not as though they were, and whatever He says comes to pass.* In Peter's heart he finds the resolve to have this peculiar interaction with the Master. "Lord, if it be You, bid me come." Jesus replies without hesitation, "Come." If you notice, Jesus did not comment on or even consider the storm that was still raging, nor its consequences. He did not tell Peter he was still young in the faith and it would take some time for him to acquire the kind of faith that would allow his mind to rise above a storm. Jesus knew the power of truth and that the consequence of the mixture of faith and His Word occupying the heart was powerful enough to calm any storm and rise above any situation. What Peter was requesting of the Lord was that word. That word would allow him to thrive in this state of affairs. He needed a foundational word, the word that would give him something to stand on and something for which to aim. He understood that he needed a word from the mouth of God to proceed in the will of God, thus fulfilling God's desire.

Man has been missing the element of God's properly placed Word in his existence ever since the fall of Adam. God foresaw Adam's fall. When looking at Genesis 2:17, we realize God makes two declarations. One declaration is a law laced with instruction, and the other a law laced with a prophetic overtone. A predictive statement that does not preclude choice but gives indication of God's omniscience and of what the choice would be. Therefore, He says, "In the day that you eat thereof," as opposed to "If you eat of this tree, then you will surely die."

Genesis 2:17 (KJV), *"But of the tree of the knowledge of good and evil, thou shalt not eat of it: for in the day that thou eatest thereof thou shalt surely die."*

Since the fall of man, we have been walking around as dead men, void of the Word of God having the seat of authority in our lives. It is the Word of God that gives us godly life, allowing us to participate in and accomplish godly things. Everything started in our journey with a word. *I cannot make a godly step without it; I cannot make a godly move if I do not hear from You, God. Lord, give me a word to stand on. A word that fixes the condition of my heart and allows Your man to operate in the manner You purposed. Give me a word to walk by. A word that illuminates my way and navigates my next step at Your direction. A word that will defy and conquer every engagement and situation that You have*

*not ordained in my life. A word that will bring down every imag-
ination, every high thing, and every vain thought that attempts to
exalt itself against and above the knowledge of God. A word that
will bring the will and power of God to supply whatever is needed
to allow me to stand and rise above every storm and tread upon
anything and everything that desires to engulf, enslave, mislead, or
consume me. With a word from the Lord, I will never sink. God...
give me a word.* Peter heard, "Come."

We, as God's people, must realize the genesis of all we
hope for and all we realize in our lives start with a word. It is within the constraints of the word that we exist and exercise that existence. "*For in him we live, and move, and have our being*" (Acts
17:28, KJV). In Him, living the word, in Him moving within its
righteous boundaries, and in Him having those things that be not as
though they were. We speak and declare in faith the word to its existence and its realization and manifestation in the physical world.

Just as the ears of darkness heard "let there be light" and
were compelled to move and let light be, so Peter heard Jesus
speak the word "come." Without a word from God, there is no next
move, no next favor, no next faith. God's word precedes what it

creates, enlightens, reveals, exposes, empowers, binds, and makes free, builds up, holds up, or tears down. His word is Him, and He is His word. Immutable and omnipotent. Once spoken, the word becomes "I am" in the lives of those to which it is delivered. The effectiveness of God's word is indisputable. What He speaks is. His every utterance produces without fail what is spoken. Therefore, to speak what He speaks is to speak certainty. God holds the patent on speaking by faith and receiving what you have spoken. God is the originator, the Word of God, and the copyright holder of everything that was created. Because God's Word is absolute, and in Him there is no shadow of turning. If God says black is blue, we can no longer say black is blue, but blue is blue. So whatever God says you are, you are. Whatever He says you can do, you can do. In today's vernacular, when speaking about the Word of God, you could say it like this, "It is...(*in truth*) what it is."

Peter heard, "Come." When God gives a word, it is a word that you cannot accomplish within your own capabilities, might, or intellect. The word that God speaks over and into your life sets the framework around what He alone can accomplish in and with your life. This word that He gives is a seed and a framework that has the fruit, the fulness, the masterwork locked up inside of it. The manifestation of it is hidden to be revealed in God's timing.

Hebrews 11:3 (KJV):

"Through faith we understand that the worlds were framed by the word of God, so that things which are seen were not made of things which do appear."

Your world and all of God's creation have borders that the Word of God has established. These you should walk within and not stray outside of or away from. Prophecies and prayers have gone forth on your life to protect you and guide you to a place and time where a real decision can be made. Consider you are where you are because your steps are ordered by the Word, and God has placed you in this place of opportunity. David said in Psalm 119, "Thy word, oh Lord, have I hid in my heart so that I might be indoctrinated by it and transformed into it so that I may repel the idea to sin against You." Not only should we hide the Word in our hearts, but we should put the Word on like a garment so that the life of Christ might be seen and our own ways, opinions, and thoughts be hidden from the world's view. Cloaked in the truth of God's Word, wrapped up in the righteousness of it—the glory of it that our nakedness and our shame is hidden from the world, and the beauty of it presented and pleasing to God. It is in this blessed position you can place confident faith in the God who speaks and what He has spoken. Faith that what He says is absolute, finished, and settled in heaven. The Word is true to the point that not a dot or title will be unfulfilled. Those who have access to the Word and trust in, rely on, and continue in it experience the freedom that is in Christ. Free to let God have His way in our life as we relinquish our way. Free to exercise and realize all the rights in Him we have according to the Word of God. This is the victory that we have in Jesus, even our faith.

Faith that comes by hearing the Word and works by love (your commitment to continuing in Him).

He can now color in the blank spots and continue His artistic endeavor, brushing on the hues of color and texture, step by each meticulous step, revealing His purpose to you and His master-piece to the world. It is a personal statement to us when the Word says, *"We are His workmanship, created in Christ Jesus unto good works"* (Ephesians 2:10, KJV).

Lord, give us the spiritual fortitude to stand still and be the canvas that You use to create Your likeness within the outline and framework You have spoken over our lives. Give us the patience to wait on You so that we see Your great salvation and men see the familiarity of the artistry, which reveals Your hand in the creation and manifestation of another masterpiece that looks like You (*the Artist*).

When first received, God's word for your life seems far-fetched, almost impossible, unseeable, outside of the realm of reason. So hard, it seems, to fit this word you know to be from God into your psyche. Certainly, what God proposes is improbable from the world's point of view. We are ill-equipped for the fulfillment of the Lord's vision for us and have little insight on the logistics of bringing the Lord's undertaking to fruition. Our faith, long-suffering, love, peace, joy, temperance, goodness, and gentleness lack maturity. So many who have felt this way have faith this way instead and found good success. For instance, Moses' deliverance of Israel from Egyptian bondage, Joshua's conquest that delivered the promised land to the children of Israel, Abraham's receiving his son Isaac at one hundred years old and through the dead womb of Sarah, Noah's ark, David's kingship, just to name a few. All of these received what looked like an impossible word, but the word was spoken by God, mixed with faith, and believed on in the heart. With each obeyed step, the life of the believer bore a greater resemblance to God's word until its full manifestation. From the power that only God possesses, God fulfilled His word in every one of those scenarios. Their victory and successes looked like God's.

The power of a word is performance. God watches over His word to perform it, producing what is spoken through His power of creativity, sheer force, influence, authority, or connectivity. The power of influence is persuading one by a convincing argument or proclamation. A truth that cannot be denied or debated. Paul said that he was persuaded in such a fashion that nothing could separate him from the love of God. The power of the word of God to perform is anchored in God's faith in His own ability to produce what He says. For us to know Him, the Lord has given us His testimony. It is called the Bible. It relates to us who He is, what He is, His character, His power, and His will to us and for us.

The God of heaven is asking us to trust Him and His Word, to believe His testimony. His Word has gone out, and He declares that it will not return to Him void. It will accomplish, fulfill, and make everything comply with the will of the One who spoke it. If we will trust Him, rest in Him, and commit to a step, keeping our eyes stayed on Him, glory will be the result of patience. Then another step. Do not worry—He is watching, watching like a father coaxing his child to take their first step. He will not let you fall; He will catch you up and repeat the process until you step, walk, run, leap, and fly with confidence. God Himself is committed to the fulfillment of His Word in the lives of those who are committed to Him. He will not let His edicts, promises, declarations, and decrees fall to the ground or return to Him void. The Word will and cannot fail. It will accomplish that which it is sent to accomplish.

Do you have a God-centered word on your life? If the answer is yes, you should cry out right where you are, "Thank You, Jesus, and glory to God." If it is not clear to you that you have a God-centered word on your life, look to heaven and speak to God, "Because I know that You are committed to Your word, Lord God, give me clarity on what You would have me to do. I need a word. I do not know how You are going to fulfill the demand You have placed on my life, God, but I submit to Your will, and I commit my way to You, to this step, and whatever You say—I will do it. I will be like Peter; waves crashing, wind swirling, rain surging, and yet I will find the resolve to do what You say and choose to take a step out of whatever boat I find myself in. I know that it takes something to step out of a boat, out of your comfort zone, complacency, addiction, fear, a toxic relationship, the storm of sickness or financial ruin, in the middle of a storm in the middle of deep water. I will not let the boat of limitations deter my walk of faith with You. The facts will state their position, but my reliance is in God stating the truth, and I will have the audacity to choose the truth and believe that I can walk above the very thing that otherwise would consume me.

Peter had a word. "Come." Do you? To move forward in God's graces, we must keep this in our hearts and minds: *everything starts with a word.*

COMMITMENT

Philippians 3:12–13 (KJV):

Not as though I had already attained, either were already perfect: but I follow after, if that I may apprehend that for which also, I am apprehended of Christ Jesus.

Brethren, I count not myself to have apprehended: but this one thing I do, forgetting those things which are behind, and reaching forth unto those things which are before, I press.

What Paul was referring to in this passage of Scripture was the pursuit of the fulfillment of the word of God in his life. Christ's likeness was something to be attained through focusing on and following after in perpetuity. That word is what we set our aim on for placement. Commitment to follow after God (who is His Word) and holding the word in the same place of His heart, with the same fervor and excitement as when he first believed, allowed God to be magnified in his life. Paul followed God step by step toward attaining his goal of being like Christ. We commit to follow the word, to take hold of the word, that the word will take root and take hold of us until we are transformed in mind to it and conformed to the image of Christ by it.

It is like using a magnifying glass to set a piece of paper on fire. You hold the magnifying glass at a particular angle to direct and intensify the ray of the sun to one place on the paper. The intensified ray becomes so hot in that area that the paper bursts into flames from the point of intensified heat. The magnifying glass has transferred the fire from the sun (its source of fire being over ninety million miles away) to the paper. Now, the fire grows and moves across every fiber of the paper offered to it, while the paper now has become the source of fire and retains that ability to transfer. The paper obtains and then retains the ability of transference until the paper is completely consumed. This is the Christian's identity, yielding ourselves to the Lord, to be set ablaze by the Holy Spirit, magnifying Jesus in the hearts of man and the world. Lights that bring illumination to dark places. In this we can see God's commitment to the words spoken in Genesis, "Let us make man."

Let us visit the two disciples that Jesus joined and accompanied on the road to Emmaus. They were in a dark place in their lives. Their fire had dwindled to a dying spark and smoldering ember that only remembered and grieved for Jesus, the Messiah, the flame of fire, the source they had been acquainted with. But when Jesus joined Himself with them as they walked along that road, the wind of his God-breathed words blew on those dying embers and set them ablaze once again. Realizing now that Jesus had been with them, their hearts burned within them as His words and presence reinforced their commitment and penetrated their innermost being.

Just as the fledgling church gathered in the upper room following the instructions of Jesus, the Holy Ghost fell upon them like tongues of fire that lit upon every one of them. We see the transferring of that fire from heaven still being magnified in the earth through our testimony. We are now that source of fire or touchstone that leads to oneness with God's fire. Oh, magnify the Lord with me, and let us exalt His name together. Spreading that flame until we ourselves, like the sacrifice that has been placed on the altar of God, have been consumed.

Second Timothy 4:6–7 (KJV):

"For I am now ready to be offered, and the time of my departure is at hand.

"I have fought a good fight, I have finished my course, I have kept the faith."

Through service we pour our lives out like a drink offering to glorify God, attending to His every word and obeying it so that our lives may yield the benefit to the kingdom the Lord desires.

The Word itself is the fuel that feeds the fire of the Holy Spirit. It is much akin to the burning bush that could not be consumed but gave its light and heat. The Word in and of itself is packed with powerful abilities and possibilities. God's Word has the ability to change things, create things, renew and revive things, edify things, heal things, and empower and glorify things, but not without commitment to it. The Word is a two-edged sword, and its cutting is determined by whether you choose it or reject it, believe it or deny it. The consequences of that Word are already determined. Your choice is the only undetermined factor in the decision-making scenario. This is God's design. But because of how God has administrated the ability of the word to perform in their life (through their decisions), it is now incumbent upon the believer to choose and commit to God (who is His Word) for the power to work or perform within their lives. Without an affirmative volunteered response to God's word, showing that the believer is committed to rising and doing what thus says the Lord, the power of a word has little authority to bring the blessing of the Lord to realization in that person's life. God's word gives the hearer a goal and a hope, something to be committed to, a reason to follow, a reason to plunge in, and a reason to let go of the world, cleave to Him, and continue to do so until the desired goal is reached. Let us explore.

A man awakes early in the morning, regardless of the time his mind found rest or his eyes knew sleep. It seems that his tenacious determination is oblivious to weather or any circumstance that occurred the night prior or the opinion of others on his comings and goings. Without missing a beat, like clockwork, he readies himself for another day of hard work. He works in a dangerous profession. He is a coal miner, a timberman in the deep mines of West Virginia. He calls it "back-breaking work" by his own definition. Because of roof falls, in the darkness of those caverns, he has been trapped and covered up numerous times. Underneath the mountains, in the blackness of those caverns, he has been pinned to the floor. Lying in distressing stillness from the pressure of fallen rock, coal, and debris pressing in on him. The sheer weight of the overburden demands each laborious breath be measured to sustain life. Lying there pondering his fate, praying for rescue, thought dead by coworkers, but by the grace of God, he emerged unscathed...this time. The possibility of peril is always present in this line of work; nevertheless, he must provide for his family. He must continue day after day, year after year, until either he becomes too old to perform the daily duties of his profession or he reaches the long-anticipated retirement age. He has seen many who shared his same toil, vision, and ambitions go prematurely by way of the grave. Nevertheless, he stays the course. In his mind's eye, he slides the faded picture from its hiding place and muses at the family he cherishes, and he beams. In that dark and perilous place, he beams with gratitude and pride. There, where his life had almost been extinguished, he finds joy in his purpose. It is in this place his pains and problems are perplexed by his peace. His care and consideration for these people fuel his drive, and their every realized and unrealized expectation, success, and joy define and energize his ambition. They depend on his love and commitment. His wife appreciates the lifestyle her husband provides, some comforts, some level of satisfaction, peace, and the security of love. He works for that. He strives to create an environment that will permit opportunities for his children to flourish, opportunities for upward movement, opportunities for them to reach in and up and attain good things, better things, growing beyond the station in life that he himself has attained to. He knows and embraces their shared expectation. Every day he toils on with these images in his view and without complaint. This is a father, and this man is obviously committed.

Then there are the athletes who train day in and day out, building upon their God-given talent, preparing themselves, and pressing to reach a certain level of strength, speed, and agility. Their hope is to make it to their chosen field of professional competition and gain an expected success. Their commitment drives them from level to level, through every opposition, laser-focused on their expectation: what they long for requires commitment's prerequisite, their self-sacrifice. They feed their bodies only the things that will promote that cause and effort. Anything that will hinder or abort this mission they disallow and refuse to subject themselves to. We all would agree that is a true athlete's journey, and their means of achieving their goals is commitment.

We see now that commitment provides the much sought-after stickability and consistency that is necessary to attain and maintain performance at the top levels of any involvement: an event, a cause, an organization, a relationship, etc. So it is within the body of Christ. It is commitment that brings us to enlightenment, illumination, edification, and a deeper and more perfect knowledge of the God we love and serve. Through the experience of consistently choosing Jesus and abiding in His Word, we grow in the experiential knowledge of Him and encounter the power that makes all things subject to His will. *"I can do all things through Christ [who strengthens] me"* (Philippians 4:13, KJV). The decision to constantly make God our priority will render all obstacles opposing us while in God's will powerless because of the power that works in us. The decision to make God first in our lives will lead us to our cherished goal of being like Him. It is the element of commitment that allows us to achieve a clearer revelation of His purpose, plan, and destiny for our lives. Commitment also moves us from the realm of uncertainty to the realm of greater faith, fellowship, communion, and relationship, where we know Him in a real biblical way, a way that defines who we are through the power of God being manifested in and through us now, and not just pointing to where we are aspiring to go. Commitment causes us to know Christ in the way that Paul describes.

Philippians 3:10 (KJV):

"That I may know Him, and the power of His resurrection, and the fellowship of His suffering, being made conformable to His death."

To the point we say, "If by any means (whatever it takes or whatever we have to offer) we may attain unto the resurrection of the dead, it will take commitment to the Word of the Lord and that Word to fill our heart and minds, empowering us, to reach that level of attainability." It is always the content of the heart that drives the intent of the heart to manifest belief. Our intent should always be Christ's likeness. A Christ-filled heart gives a life direction, sets goals to aspire to, and provides wisdom and power to make decisions that are complementary to our journey and destination. The Holy Spirit will always whisper from a surrendered heart words of unerring righteousness after the counsel of His own will.

The Bible says that Abraham was strong in faith, meaning he knew something about God, and what he knew he believed without doubt. He was willing to step out on God's Word because he believed the One who promised was faithful. That faith in the faithful came by hearing, and it was by hearing the Word of God. Abraham filled his heart with what God had promised and what He had decreed. The content of his heart drove the intent (which fueled his steps). His intent was whatever he heard God say about him. God said for him to leave his father's house, his kindred, and the land he dwelt in. Abraham intentionally left. God tells Abraham that his name is no longer Abram, but it is Abraham. Abram intentionally introduces himself as Abraham from that day forward. God tells Abraham that he is going to have a child, even when he is one hundred years old and Sarah is ninety-nine and naturally infertile. Abraham intentionally believed God over and against his circumstances. With his will, Abraham chose to step by faith into the world of the word. The world that speaks things that be not as though they were and by faith believes and declares the word into manifestation. Commitment drove the will to keep that choice in place, continually choosing God's declaration over all other assertions, expecting what God expects, and seeing and declaring what God sees and declares.

Abraham continually believed what the Lord had spoken to him. The continual choosing of what the Lord had promised fueled every step he took. The response to the choice of the will is your action, manifested belief. The step is manifested action that reveals the intent of the heart. Abraham imparted God's message into his seed after him. His expectation was the expansion of the promise through seeing his posterity experience God's plans for those who choose Him.

It is commitment that continually pushes for the thoughts that reflect God's ideas, thoughts that agree with the heart's content and build upon the heart's intent of reaching a goal or attaining completion or resolution of a desired goal. This is how Paul could say that he had fought a good fight and had finished his course... each choice empowered his step. Step by step, a walk, a way, was developed as commitment followed after, chased, or pursued the chosen word, thought, or opinion until the heart's goal was manifested...it is a true statement that "the will" will expose the content and intent of the heart through its choosing.

Gethsemane

Case in point. Jesus at Gethsemane is at war within Himself between two conflicting opinions, the will of the flesh and the will of God. He is now agonizing with the realization that He, the Son of the Most High God, is soon to be brutalized, humiliated, and meet a cruel death on a cross He by no means deserves. Nevertheless, that same cross has been reserved for Him and only Him before the foundation of the world. He knew He was innocent of any wrong, along with the knowledge that He came for this very purpose.

In my mind's eye, I can visualize the garden scenario and conversation. Jesus, in His humanity, is physically experiencing and demonstrating extreme anxiety. He is praying earnestly and fervently. The stress of His situation has Jesus sweating what seems to be great drops of blood as the pressure is mounting and the hour grows closer for Him to lay down His life. Jesus' commitment is being challenged as He utters the words, "Father, is there any other way to get this done? Any way this cup of suffering can pass by me?" Any way...any way...? Nevertheless...this is the moment of real clarity; this is the opportune moment to choose.

THE POWER OF THE CHOICE

In this nevertheless moment, thank God, we can see our choices, good and bad, for what they really are. This is the moment where choices are weighed in the balance of God's Word, and you see their intrinsic value and their long-term effect. Jesus, in this moment, had to look at the joy, the glory. He had to reflect on the purpose of why He came. This was His goal. This was His aim and His purpose. All those who would be saved through His sacrifice were before Him. The Father's glory was before Him. Victory was before Him. Satan's defeat was before Him. Obtaining the keys of death and hell was before Him. Being seated on the right hand of the throne of God was before Him. Restoration of God's man was before Him. The empowerment and coming of the kingdom of heaven on earth were before Him. The great peace of His people was before Him. All the benefits toward the children of God were before Him. The manifestation of the sons of God was before Him. Oh, what joy was before our Savior! This one act would bring the greatest glory to God and enrich the kingdom throughout the ages.

The Bible says Jesus is who we look to while we are running this race, laying aside every weight and besetting sin. While the adversarial forces of Satan are opposing every move we desire to make for Christ and it looks like the easiest solution for you is to give up, just look up to the hill from whence comes your help. Look unto Jesus, our Savior and Lord, and study how He lived His life with intent and purpose. Gazing upon the author and finisher of our faith will grow the intent and give it sustaining power.

The example that Jesus set is the following.

Hebrews 12:2 (KJV):

"Looking unto Jesus the author and finisher of our faith; who for the joy that was set before him endured the cross, despising the shame, and is set down at the right hand of the throne of God."

Jesus chose according to purpose. Jesus committed, and the Bible says He became obedient even to the death of the cross. *"Lo, I come in the volume of the book to do thy will oh God"* (Hebrews 10:7, KJV). Not a sentence or a chapter of the book but the whole volume. Jesus came to do the whole will of God. *Not my will, but Thy good and perfect will be accomplished.* In this nevertheless moment, Jesus in His humanity chose to commit, to devote Himself, His way, and His life to the whole will of the Father. Not caught up in a scene but aware of the whole story and its objective. In between His inquiry and the joy set before Him was the consistency of commitment, dedication, and the devotion to stay, to endure, to remain in obedience to the will of the Father.

I have heard that if you want to see commitment, all you have to do is look at a good country breakfast supplied with ham and eggs. In it you will understand the difference between involvement and commitment. We understand that you can walk away from involvement, but commitment will cost you everything. In the breakfast we see the chicken's contribution of the eggs and conclude the chicken was involved, seeing it supplied the eggs and walked away alive to see another day. But the pig was not so lucky; he had to be committed. This delicious breakfast that we enjoy cost him his life. As with the pig, so it is with Christ. The life, joy, peace, strength, love, righteousness, hope, favor, and acceptance from God that we enjoy cost Him His life. He was committed. Oh, taste and see that the Lord is good, and His mercy endures forever.

Inevitably we have to choose whether we are going to be involved or committed. Commitment has a defined path governed

84

by ordained words with ordained outcomes. These words influence, and this path leads to the outcomes we desire but have to be chosen and followed. Along life's journey there will be tests and trials, but be assured that there will be an ever-present God to see you through to joy.

In life we are presented with what seems like a consistent barrage of never-ending choices. Although there are many, it is only the suggestions or influences we choose that can affect our lives. The choices in our lives are like the innumerable drops of water that make up our oceans, but it is the waters that we choose, the waters that we interact with and indulge in (the rivers, lakes, showers, baths, faucets, the glasses of drinking or cooking waters, etc.) that define and fulfill our desires and needs, that satisfy the intent of our heart and become a part of our life experience. We immerse ourselves in the water the will chooses, and commitment compels the will to continually choose that water as often as the need or desire for its application presents itself. We become committed to its continual involvement and result.

Likewise, choices are presented in the form of words that form thoughts. These thoughts are so prevalent that we think of

THE POWER OF THE CHOICE

them in many cases like we think of air. We know that an abundance of air is present, but because of its easy access and constant being there, we dismiss the thought of thinking about every breath. We inhale and exhale almost subconsciously, our bodies acting on only the air that was breathed in; our body is committed to breathing and processes the gift of oxygen, allowing it to become a part of our existence. In a few seconds, we exhale—releasing the depleted breath that we had taken in seconds before, only to repeat the process. We take in new oxygen-rich air so that we might continue breathing, growing, progressing, and continue living. Our bodies continually choose air. Nothing else will suffice and sustain us. Nothing else will qualify to give us the fullness of life that we yearn for. Just as air gives life to the body, it is in Christ that we live and move and have our being. It is His Word we should choose to breathe in daily. Every day, every moment, we must choose to breathe Him into our being: a sip of living water, a breath of life, a word of hope and power, a thought that will become a part of our life experience, our steps, our way, and an established path. This should be every child of God's choice and commitment.

Even when we do not choose, we have chosen. Some have

become weary with the possibilities and have no deliberation in their choices; whatever comes their way—anything goes, carelessness. Some continually choose evil or self; a forward man, a transgressor. Some choose the good for a while and then find pleasure for a season in choosing evil. They cannot make up in their minds what they want to be committed to, or maybe they have. The Bible calls this double-minded or hypocritical. But God is looking for the man who will agree with making Him and His Word their continual habitation and constant choice. A single-eyed, single-minded man, the Bible calls the individual who will make God their priority. This is the man who God will shower His blessings upon and withhold no good thing from. A man whose steps are ordered by the Lord because he has chosen wisdom. The voice of the Lord is his guide, and every word spoken a compass to direct each step. His ear rests on the heart of God, passionately seeking direction for every area in his life. Forsaking emotion's cry to lead, this man instead commits to following and pleasing God with his love, worship, and obedience to God's Word.

To experience God's *soteria (His so great salvation)* daily, we must be steadfastly devoted to God's Word. Continually

THE POWER OF THE CHOICE

preferring Him and His instructions moves us from this level of

testing and trial to victory, the next level of sacrifice to provision

and prosperity, from humility to glory, obtaining greater faith

and experiencing a more perfect knowledge of God's person, His

presence, His power, and His promise in our everyday walk. This

is what Jesus meant when the Word said, *"Then Jesus said to those*

Jews [that] believed on Him, if [you] continue in my word [to

choose the Word moment to moment, daily walking in it], then are

[you] my disciple indeed, and [you] shall know the truth [perceive

it, realize it and its manifestation] and the truth [will] make you

free [release you from thinking like the world, approaching life's

problem from a flesh-centered philosophy—free from being bound

to what only this world offers and free to explore and experience

the vastness of God's power, presence, and graces now]" (John

8:31–32, KJV). The fruit of your commitment is God's revealed

favor as He elevates you in the knowledge of Him. This is what

Paul desired and what we experience as we mature in Christ. In

comparison to what he had found in Jesus, he counted all things

that he possessed or had attained in this world but rubbish that

he might win Christ. He pursued a greater knowledge of Christ,

88

laser-focused on Him, and was committed to living a life that was consistent with the words that Mary told the servants in John 2:1–11 while attending the wedding in Cana, *"Whatsoever he saith unto you, do it"* (John 2:5, KJV).

To illustrate this, we can look at Jesus during His temptation in the wilderness when the Bible says he was hungered. The devil challenged Jesus' core belief by suggesting that He turn the stone into bread. He was suggesting to Jesus to act on the will of the adversary and willfully place a malignant word (a word that Satan presented) in the place within His heart that God's word occupied. Friend, please understand that Satan knows how God's word works. His suggestion was evil and devilish. For a miracle to happen in that scenario, Jesus' intent would have to look past the miracle and focus on the word giver. Jesus would have to look away from what the Father had spoken and look to Satan. His suggestion to Jesus was to commit treason against His Father by replacing God's word with the word of Satan. Jesus replied that man should not live by bread alone but by every word that proceeds out of the mouth of God (*God's words*). In other words, I choose God's words, God's thoughts, to remain in my heart and

THE POWER OF THE CHOICE

not another. I recognize the fingerprint of pride and selfishness. I see the footprint of deception, the one who has exploited the weakness and vulnerabilities of the lust of the flesh, the lust of the eye, and the pride of life. I know your tactic is to bombard me with words during what you deem as a weak and susceptible time in my life. I am aware you are the enemy and wish to formulate and place thoughts in my mind that are contrary to what my Father says. But I still choose God and God's words, God's thoughts, because I am committed to seeing the manifestation of the intents of His heart for me and through me. This is the truth I believe in, that I cling to. That is why I press. Therefore, I push. Therefore, I hold the line; I stand. I hide this word (God's thoughts) in my heart so that I might not sin against Him. I don't frustrate the grace God provided me. I know that His thoughts are continually good toward me, and I have an expected end because His word is settled in the center of my being. I have become His word through obedience. What He has spoken into my life I am. Commitment has required an investment of me. That I empty myself and be infused with the life-sustaining power of the word. *"Though he slay me yet will I trust Him"* (Job 13:15, KJV). Though He devours my earthly life, I offer it up to

Him to His glory. Yet, I will trust, rely on, and have faith in Him all the days of my life until my change comes.

The devil tries Jesus twice more in this scenario. Seeing Jesus' commitment and hearing His declarations, the devil leaves Him. The devil sees a powerhouse, a true Son of God, and leaves Him. There is nothing that he can do with One who is full of the Word and committed to doing the will of God. Just like Jesus.

But what does the world see when someone is fully persuaded and committed to God in this day and time? When they are praying every day without ceasing, looking to heaven, and crying out to God, what does the world see? What do people see when one is constantly in the Word, seeking the wisdom that leads to eternal life? What does the world see when these souls refuse to conform to societal norms that challenge their spiritual goals? The way that the world responds to life is devoid of God and yet still viewed as relevant.

In the days of Daniel, when the Babylonian society normalized the bowing down and worshipping the idol of the king, to the godly, this was distasteful and willfully rejected. Shadrach, Meshach, and Abednego chose rather to approach life by way of the Word and suffer the reproach of the king, choosing God's ideologies and responses to life's challenges and offerings while being denigrated by unregenerated men. Committed is not what these heroes of faith are called. They are called fanatics, crazy, fools, misinformed, Bible thumpers, holy rollers, strange, confused. Some may have called the Hebrew boys toast and a host of other defamatory titles. Committed was not one of them. But committed is what they were. The Bible tells us in Hebrews 12:3 (KJV) we should "*consider him that endured such contradiction of sinners against himself, lest ye be wearied and faint in your minds.*" It was Him and the martyrs of this world that resisted unto blood, striving against sin. They were committed.

Often, we do not recognize commitment when we see it. It is often misread, then misrepresented, and sometimes mistreated. Commitment's obviousness is sometimes hidden by the needed actions that must be taken to ensure the desired end or outcome. For instance, chastisement is often the means by which the favorable outcome of obedience and good behavior are realized. But the onlooker nor the one being chastised would agree that during that punishment, the actions they witnessed or endured were promoted by commitment. I must interject right here and make everyone aware that I have witnessed this kind of commitment personally. I am here to tell you today my mother, Pastor Rocine Jackson, was committed! I say this humorously, but the statement is overflowing in truth.

Commitment is consistently making the same choice. It is the choice that determines direction. Commitment is the element (zeal—devotion) that you apply that causes you to stick, stay, endure, and be tenacious in your perseverance. Commitment stabilizes the steps of belief, and each step taken produces more confidence and strength. With each decision we make for God, commitment proves we are all in and live by every word that proceeds out of the mouth of God, and every word proves itself to be true through the manifested goodness of our Lord. He supplies, He protects, He heals, He saves. God does all these things and more for His children. We demonstrate daily we are committed to and love our God when we serve Him in obedience with our strength, time, and talents. He becomes more important than the rich young ruler's "all we have." Commitment goes deeper than the dime; it goes to the devotion of the heart. We present our bodies as a living

THE POWER OF THE CHOICE

sacrifice, holy and acceptable to God, and this is just reasonable. We commit our minds to transformation, our hands to service, and our hearts to worship; no opinion or thought is higher than that of our Savior. Our steps are committed to His order and His command, and no other life journey has a more sure or anticipated destination, no endeavor has loftier goals, no life sweeter, no love more enduring, and no involvement more rewarding.

Father, we pray right now that You help us to remove the clutter from our lives and commit our whole heart to You. Help us so that our heart becomes more occupied by Your Word, resulting in our intent mirroring You, the content of our hearts. We surrender the entirety of who and what we are to You so that Your will be accomplished in and with our lives. Thank You for clarity to see ourselves as not already attaining but following Your every command so that we are steadfast and immovable…always abounding in Your work. We will see that work to completion and will not be ashamed or abated from it. Help us to always bring glory and honor to Your name, forever committed. In the precious name of Jesus, we pray. Amen.

94

THE PRODUCT OF COMMITMENT IS PERMANENCE

John 12:24 (KJV), *"Verily, verily, I say unto you, except a corn of wheat fall into the ground and die, it abideth alone: but if it die, it bringeth forth much fruit."*

We have discussed choices in chapter 1, placement of the virtue pursuing word in chapter 2, the genesis of everything, which starts with a word in chapter 3, and commitment in chapter 4, and now we want to shed light on and bring insight to commitment's product, which is permanence.

THE POWER OF THE CHOICE

We have established that the placement of God's Word is vital, but placement alone is not enough. The continuity of the manifested Word in the life of the believer is contingent upon keeping the Word perfectly placed in your heart. The seed must fall to the ground and remain. Consider the seed the Word of God, the ground the heart of the believer, and the condition to experience fruitfulness is that it remains in place. The emphasis is on the keeping, committing it there, holding it fast, and meditating on it day and night, allowing the Word to saturate, work, and produce itself in our everyday walk.

We must work the Word like working a garden for it to yield or produce for us. I remember seeing my father gardening when I was young.

Oftentimes he would enlist my help to create and tend the garden. Now that I look back on it, I wasn't much help, but he was depositing truth in my life that I can glean understanding and guidance even in this day. It was interesting how he would plow the fallowed ground and prepare it to receive seed. Sometimes he employed a mule and plow. Now that was a sight to see. I remember the smell of the broken earth, almost sweet to the senses. I know now that I didn't see what he saw when he was preparing for planting. I could only see the process, but he saw the product. His determination, spurred by his intent, was evident, as he would get home from a long day of working in the coal mines, and foregoing rest, he would immediately go to work in his garden. He saw the harvest, the outcome, the product, and the joy when I could only focus on the process, procedure, and method. His vision was the catalyst to his steadfastness in getting the seed into good ground. Anything that was not conducive to the process of growing the seed was removed from the garden. Rocks and weeds were not tolerated but quickly plucked out and thrown aside. Bugs and vermin that would devour the seed in its earliest development were dissuaded as well. Likewise, even when the plants were developing throughout the growing and harvesting seasons, he still monitored and removed nutrient-stealing weeds to give our seeds the greatest opportunity to produce the expected harvest.

He was committed to seeing the full manifestation of the seed.

As true believers, the question we should ask ourselves is, "Are we doing everything possible to allow the seed of the Word to have its full manifestation in our lives?" Do we have that kind of foresight and fortitude that expects and ensures a heart environment that is conducive for the maximum output from the Word of God? If we were honest, the answer would be no. The parable of the sower applies here in this portion of our writing. I do not believe that most Christians' hearts fall under the definition of stony ground in the parable of the sower, but I do believe that many have allowed the cares of this life to choke the seed, reducing the seed's ability to show forth the richness of the kingdom of God in the saints, in its full glory, to the world. I believe this is the reason God has assigned the writing of this book. It is to remind us of the fervor we had when we were first saved. To make us aware that we have stopped choosing Him continually and sincerely. We say His praise shall continually be in our mouth, but many of us can recall several times that this was just not true. The lengths we used to go to please God. The sacrifices we would make to ensure that He and His will were priority in our lives and that our actions brought a smile of acceptance to the face of our God. We were committed. It was until death do us part.

Hebrews 2:1 (KJV), *"Therefore we ought to give the more*

earnest heed to the things which we have heard, lest at any time we should let them slip."

The more earnest heed is the relationship with the Word that the scripture is calling for. There is a monitoring and guarding of the invested seed, making sure the Word takes root to ensure the operation of permanence is active. We can place the Word there, but there must be a committing, watering, weeding, burying, hiding, and guarding so it will flourish in its manifestation. We must not miss another opportunity and veto the moment for the Word to have that God-revealing, man-enlightening manifestation. The committing: The family gathers around the grave in which the body of their dear mother will soon be buried and for some time occupy. The last views have been taken, tears have been shed, songs have been sung, comments have been made, and the preacher has preached the Word. The funeral procession has relocated from the church, and they are now at the grave site. The words that will culminate the service can now be articulated, "It is tenderly and reverently that we commit this house to the grave. The body returns to the earth, from which our bodies came. The spirit returns to God, who gave it, waiting for the day when both spirit and body shall again be united at the coming of the Lord." Some flowers are chosen for keepsakes, and the casket at some point is lowered into the ground, with all intent to remain there until the coming of the Lord. There is a permanence in this act of committing. The body will stay there committed until the Lord acts. In this commitment we see a lesson to be learned in how we deal with the Word of God in our lives. Let us explore.

The permanency of commitment is not only applied to the assignment of an entity into the power of another relationship but also involves resisting the return of the committed entity's involvement in the former relationship. After a person dies and the body is committed to the grave, there is no return to the former relationship with life. Let me say it more plainly—the committed body cannot have the same relationship with those who are living because of the power of death and the grave. The relationship with the dust of the ground has power over that body. The new relationship takes precedence. That permanence is the product of commitment.

The institution of marriage can be used to illustrate this concept further. Two young people are contemplating a relationship and begin to interact with each other, having mutual interest.

The young man and woman each have their own goals, dreams, and opinions. They both have their own way, and often these ways are different in cultural content and life direction. But they find enough commonality that they involve themselves in courtship and decide to make this an exclusive relationship, and this is based on a mutual attraction. The courtship grows more serious, and engagement ensues, creating a new level of relationship instituted through mutual agreement. The marriage day is set, and the bride and groom stand before God and man and recite their vows, declaring their love and commitment to one another until death do them part. The power of commitment produces the permanence that disallows these two young people from reversion to their former relationships or any other relationship that would endanger the continuity of their vow. They have assigned their lives to one another, and the new commitment takes precedence over any other earthly relationship. The bond resists all forces that seek to break the union's vow. The sealing of the vow says it all. "*What therefore God [has] joined together let no man put asunder*" (Mark 10:9, KJV). This permanence is the product of commitment.

THE POWER OF THE CHOICE

We see in the preceding illustrations of the body being assigned or committed to the grave until the Lord acts and the uniting of the committed young couple in marriage until death do them part. The permanence and continuity of commitment are followed by the caveats of until the return of Christ and until death do us part. This implies a future relationship or assignment that can annul or supersede the prior commitment.

The Bible tells us in Hebrews 8:6 that we as believers have been given a better covenant, a stronger commitment, or assignment through and by the excellent ministry of Jesus Christ: His death, burial, and resurrection. The gospel of grace is the covenant or commitment that supersedes the prior by strength, quality, righteousness, justice, and longevity. The better assignment has been sealed with the precious blood of Jesus Christ. Jesus committed Himself to the cross and remained there until death, satisfying the judgment of God against man. The punishment of death had been carried out on One that had the same unblemished standing that Adam possessed before the fall. Thereby being the perfect and only sacrifice that could have been offered to free man from the bounds of his former sentence. Jesus was committed to being that Lamb of God so that we might be made the sons of God. It is now our responsibility to believe that Christ has died, was buried, risen from the dead, ascended to glory, and now is seated at the right hand of the throne of God. He is offering us the gift of grace so that we might know God and experience Him daily. It is Christ that has given humanity the ability to rise from that fleshly grave in the newness of life, freeing our spirits by the application of His own blood. It is Christ's commitment that has purchased the permanence of life, joy, and peace. It is Christ's commitment that has produced the permanent right for us to put on the robe of righteousness and be called the sons of God. It is the commitment of Christ that has produced the permanence of our sins being forgiven and cast into the sea of forgetfulness, never to be remembered again. The product of commitment is permanence. It is our responsibility to believe God and commit our way to Him for the results and promises of the Word to become the realities in our lives. We commit our work to Him, and He will establish our ways. This refers to the assigning of our ways, our own way, the world's way to a place where the committed becomes still until another act is instituted. What is the other act? The Lord said that He would act. Placing the Word in our heart and committing our way to Him allows God to work in us to will and to do His good pleasure. In our presenting our bodies as a living sacrifice, holy and acceptable unto God, we are allowing God to produce His life in us so that it will be walked out in our everyday life. We are committing our former lives to be buried with Christ and rising in newness of Christ's life. Daily this life becomes more evident through the transforming power of the Holy Spirit as we choose each moment to die to our own way and allow God to have His. Do this, and God will make the product of the Word permanent in your life.

Jesus committed and submitted to the cross to turn the defeat that we experienced daily into victory, turn hopelessness to a living hope, and turn faith into the substance of that hope evidenced by revelation. Faith in what Christ has accomplished for us is the victory. A real, tangible victory that we can experience through the Word in perpetuity if we truly commit our way and our work to Him. If this is the permanence that you desire, Christ died so that you could freely possess it and possess it more abundantly.

WISDOM

Wisdom is the principal thing...

He has become reckless in his living. Many nights, it is after 3:00 a.m. when he comes home...*if* he comes home. Showing up reeking of the smell of alcohol or marijuana, accompanied by his inability to focus and his stagger, has become a frequent and distasteful occurrence. Looking from the outside in, you would think all that he has been taught and all he has seen with his own eyes has escaped him. The wrong road that he had been warned of has found appeal in his eyes, and that road he has welcomed. His new life counselors (masquerading as friends or vice versa) and their influences have superseded good counsel and sound judgment. He has become a prodigal, unprofitable, and if something is not done soon, the likely probability is he will become a liability and source of pain and grief to his family through perils that would certainly befall him. Worst case scenario, he could become an added number to one of those dreaded statistics of imprisonment or deaths that happen far too often in too many communities that look like his.

THE POWER OF THE CHOICE

His father knows him, and perhaps his father recognizes a glimpse of himself in the young man. His capabilities and potential have been pointed out by many. He has no problem with school-work; he is of more than average intelligence, although he only does just a little more than enough to get by. He has a pleasant personality and gets along well with others. He will work hard at what he loves or has an interest in. Most things outside of that bore him. He is an avid reader and reads almost anything. His oldest sister gave him a small library of books when he was in the fifth grade. Her only prerequisite was he make good grades. To him that was no problem. This sparked his love of reading and striving to understand what his mind had been introduced to. He has just about read them all and some more than once. Baseball is his thing, but he can excel in other sports as well. So with all of this going for him, why the drugs, drinking, and wild living? Why does he choose to abandon his spiritual teachings and wildly go after a crowd whose end has been foretold and is foreseeable to any and everyone but him? He has become a prodigal, and a prodigal does not operate in wisdom but in selfishness.

Wisdom, in the simplest of definitions, is insight for living, along with the ability to make the right choices for good based on those insights. In the Old Testament, the Hebrew captures the whole of wisdom in two words: *Chokma*, which denotes the knowledge of nature and human affairs and the skill or ability to perceive and foretell the future. *Tushiya* combines well-being with wisdom and is interpreted as sound wisdom. In James 3 we are told of a wisdom that comes from above. The Bible tells us to seek this wisdom out, and if we lack it, ask God, who gives it liberally and holds nothing back. This wisdom is spoken about in Proverbs 8, and the many attributes of wisdom are noted. Wisdom declares to be the first formed attribute of God and was there when all creation was being laid out. Wisdom cries out to all humanity to seek it, follow it, embrace it, and possess it.

Proverbs 8:35–36 (KJV):

"For whoso findeth me findeth life, and shall obtain favour of the LORD.

"But he that sinneth against me wrongeth his own soul: all they that hate me love death."

The Word says that Christ has made unto us wisdom. It

THE POWER OF THE CHOICE

is something that He desires you to have because, in possessing wisdom, you will be led to Him, causing you to make the right decisions and bringing you prosperity in all areas of life: your spirit, soul, and body. In other words, the godly kind of wisdom leads you to the truth, and as you continue walking in the truth, truth will make you free.

Balance

Wisdom is also instrumental in bringing balance to your life. This concept is interesting to me because of the way the Lord revealed it. Wisdom is knowing how to resist evil and perform well. Knowing this, we must also consider wisdom has to be chosen.

While having a phone conversation with my nephew DJ, he presented a philosophical and biblical truth concerning the balance between evil and good in the world. At first hearing, his statement and question were intriguing to me, and although it rang with truth, there seemed to be something that needed to be delved into for us to acquire a fruitful understanding. Thus, the statement, "There is a balance in the world of good and evil. Because we live in the world, we must encounter these two elements daily and find the balance in our everyday living." What was said was so true and caused me to meditate just on that. His questions, "With so much of each in the world, in order to maintain balance, which side do you run to? What role do we play in the balancing, and what are the effects of running to either side?" It did not take long before the Holy Spirit quickened an answer in my spirit. I explained that though evil and good do exist in the world and the knowledge of them, there is a divine process that allows an individual to deal with the scale of good and evil correctly, thereby maintaining balance. It is a truth that the stabilizing force that maintains balance does its work within an individual's life, and that same balance is manifested in the world. I asked the question, "What do the evil and the good balance on?" He was somewhat baffled by the question, but when the answer came, his eyes were opened. Truth is the entity that keeps good and evil balanced. The evil and the good had to balance on something, and that something was the truth.

There had to be an entity that set in the middle and divided the evil and the good and rightly distributed the theoretical weight of each side. That element had to be truth. Truth (the Word) is constantly in the middle. So my answer was (in order to keep balance), "Don't run to the good or the evil but rather run to the middle." God did not send His Son into the world to condemn or judge the world but to save the world through the truth. Jesus is the truth that balances the knowledge of good and evil in the human condition. He alone had conquered and overcome the world when He lived a perfect life, walking in truth while resisting evil and performing well. He never ran toward the good things or the evil, but we find Him always gravitating to the Father's will in every situation in His life.

It is not wise to run to or place undue value on the things of evil or the things of good. Things, giftings, anointings, blessings, concepts, attitudes, prosperity, healing, tongues, or any other thing cannot attain the favor of God for you. But rather run to and embrace the truth, run to Jesus, who has been made wisdom, and He will give you the ability to choose wisely and maintain the truth without being overwhelmed by things, whether good or evil.

The Bible says that the love of money is the root of all evil, yet it declares that if we seek the kingdom of God and all His righteousness, all the other things will be added to us. We have fought the fight against the prosperity preachers. Yet the Bible says through Paul that he would like that we prosper and be in health even as our souls are prospered. There is no contradiction here. The love of money is the root of all evil—not money but the love of it. The mishandling of fire may be the root to your house burning down, but fire is not the culprit. It is the *mishandling* of an entity that is here to do us good that has caused that calamity. The inordinate affection you place on a thing makes it a detriment to you.

It is true that men often run after good things with a fervor that does not exist when running after God. That is not prosperity. God is saying that if you want balance and your desire is to please Him, "*seek ye first the kingdom of God and all His righteousness and all [other] things [will] be added to you*" (Matthew 6:33, KJV). He is the only One that can show you how to exist in a world and enjoy the richness, fullness, and the fruit of it while wholly magnifying Him and keeping Him the priority in your life. In other words, He will show you how to resist the evil inclination and perform the good instruction through firmly embracing the truth, which allows you to enjoy the richness of the kingdom through obedience. This is wisdom. Please examine the

111

THE POWER OF THE CHOICE

charts presented on the following page to give you a visual of the concepts we are discussing in the text.

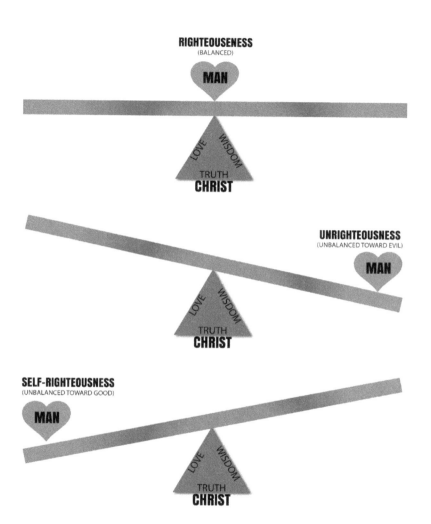

THE POWER OF THE CHOICE

In the beginning, God knew Adam and Eve were not yet prepared to handle the weight of the knowledge of good and evil. Presented this mammoth of a package by an unauthorized source, they were crushed under the vastness of it. Since they were ill-prepared to balance this weighty task, their fascination and imagination had not been conditioned enough to deal with the endless possibilities, whether good or evil. They lived in the dispensation of innocence, and they were the innocent children of God. Therefore, God forbade them to eat of that fruit for their own protection. This was the law that governed that dispensation. God's decree, *"For in the day that thou eatest thereof thou shalt surely die."* (Genesis 2:17, KJV). Wisdom gave them the ability to make the right choice, and if they kept this truth in their hearts (commitment), their world was balanced. When that Word ceased to be the priority in their lives, when God's Word was displaced, the proof was manifested that they were not ready to handle the knowledge the tree provided. Their balance moved to evil and away from God when His Word ceased to be their authority and His presence ceased to be their intent and contentment. Their action allowed sin access and death entered by sin. We can see sin manifesting itself in doubt, rebellion, willfulness, pride, flesh, nakedness, and death, all in this one setting. The communication with the serpent influenced Adam and Eve to reject God and grant sin access into the heart and mind of man, fulfilling the word that God had spoken previously. "In the day that you eat thereof..." It is a true statement that evil communications corrupt good manners.

It is hard to speak of wisdom and not touch on Solomon, who was considered the wisest man who ever lived on this planet apart from Jesus. His special brand of wisdom extracted truth from almost any situation. This wisdom also gained him great wealth and glory. Around the known world, he was revered because of the great wisdom that he had been afforded from God and the great treasures he had amassed because of that wisdom. Even to this day, the wisdom of Solomon is an alternative expression for right decisions and seeking out and extracting profitable truths.

If wisdom is the tool used to expose truth and give the ability to make the right choices, why do men not chase after wisdom, desire it, and cling to it? In the Gospel of John, when speaking of God, it says that the Word became flesh. Jesus has many names and titles: the Word, the Truth, the Light, the Son of God, Wisdom.

THE POWER OF THE CHOICE

Therefore, we can say without fallacy that Wisdom became flesh and dwelt among us. Jesus is the last Adam that made the right choices. He is the way (by which we obtain), the truth (the center of balance in choosing), and the light (illumination, enlightenment) that we seek after and run to that brings balance in our lives and makes everything as it should be. *"The name of the Lord is a strong tower; the righteous run into it, and we are safe"* (Proverbs 18:10, NIV). He is the truth that makes us free. Underneath His wings we find rest and safety. Run to Him. Scripture bears it out; the more we gravitate toward God, the more our lives are balanced and whole. The center never moves. We must move to the center of His will. He is like the Rock of Gibraltar. He is the same yesterday, today, and forever. He is the standard by which our lives are governed and the wisdom by which we discern how to shun evil and perform good. Therefore, we must move to Him, move to the center of our joy, the fulfillment and balance of our lives. Jesus Christ.

Isaiah 59:19 (KJV), *"So shall they fear the name of the Lord from the west, and his glory from the rising of the sun. When the enemy shall come in like a flood, the Spirit of the Lord shall lift up a standard against him."*

That standard is Jesus. That standard is truth. The standard is wisdom.

What about the prodigal we started this chapter with? The prodigal has gone through many things in his life. His involvement in a horrific car accident at the age of seventeen resulted in the loss of one of his closest friends. He and his friend had been transported to the hospital and placed in the same room. While lying on the gurney, he could hear William gasping for each breath. Lying there, he watched as the doctors and nurses worked franticly over William's body to no avail. He watched helplessly as his friend took his very last breath, and in this world, in a moment, his friend was no more. That memory never left him and never got easier to bare.

Married at twenty-two and divorced at twenty-seven. He thought he was ready for marriage. God warned him; his father warned him, and his own conscience warned him, and still, he went his own way into the failed union. No blame on his former spouse, but all goes to not listening and choosing what the Lord was speaking to his heart, but he ignored. Since he was estranged from his two children, his life was in turmoil, and all he could think of was the blessed life his mother and father had enjoyed

117

in Christ and how much his life did not resemble theirs. He remembers when he was going his own way and looking through the dining room window of the family church as a teenager. In the sanctuary, his father was lying on the altar praying at midday, crying out to the Lord to bless his son. He remembers often coming home from school for lunch as a grade-schooler to find his mother kneeling before the Lord, caught up in the fervency of prayer. It was a surety that they had problems in their lives, but they had the wisdom to know they possessed something bigger, more powerful, more alluring than their problems. They had a love, a center, a rock, a strong tower, a standard that they could go to that brought balance to their lives, and that balance he desires.

The witness of his mother and father is the truth that he hoped to be to his children. Those two living epistles help the young man make up his mind to return to the Lord. He is tired of being exposed to the pain of disobedience, the ridicule of the world, the echoes of defeat and regret, of failure. He is tired of the hardness and toil of the transgressor's way, the course that off-center bad decisions have made for him. He repents and cries out to the Lord to forgive and deliver him, reverencing God's wisdom, power, and ability to save, deliver, and make free. Without hesitation, the Lord hears, forgives, receives, and restores him into the center of truth. He is now balanced. He has made the right choice. The fear of living life without Christ motivates him to run to the center. This is the beginning of wisdom.

Proverbs 9:10 (AMP):

The [reverent] fear of the LORD [that is, worshiping Him and regarding Him as truly awesome] is the beginning and the preeminent part of wisdom [its starting point and its essence], And the knowledge of the Holy One is understanding and spiritual insight.

Wisdom is the primary thing. Let us make this plain by declaring that wisdom is the main thing, the most important, the primary, the basic, the key thing, the head, the leader. Wisdom was so important to God that Jesus became wisdom to us because He knew that man's capability of holding on to it and following after it was poor. The beginning of wisdom is the fear of the Lord, but man chose not to keep God in his knowledge. Wisdom is essential, something that God could not afford we miss, mess up, and make the mistake of not taking hold of. Therefore, the Lord packaged His wisdom in Jesus and gave it as a gift to us. He gave us a perfect life in Christ, the overcoming of the world through perfect choices that dealt with good and evil in the correct way. That always choose God's will, even to the death of the cross. He gave us wisdom in a pleasing sacrifice, locked it up in a mystery, hid it from the adversary, revealed it to us, and presented it to a just God, settling our unpayable debt with His own blood. Wisdom became our sin and was nailed to a cross. By the blood of His cross, Wisdom conquered death and the grave, defeated sin, gave us His victory and filled us with His Spirit, and cloaked us in His righteousness, which granted us access into His presence once again. Wisdom is offered to all so that we might experience that victory and power supplied to us every day through the indwelling of the Holy Spirit in the heart of the believer. When I look at Jesus and all He carried out while in the flesh, yes…I see the wisdom of God in such a clear, transparent, and powerful way. Before the foundation of the world, it was in the mind of God how He was going to redeem mankind. God, being omniscient and knowing the end from the beginning, housing all wisdom in His own mind, sent Jesus, His own Son, into the world to accomplish this for us. God

Himself came in the flesh for sin so He could redeem humanity and give us a gift that filled our every need, providing what we lacked, and He did that from a supply He has an abundance of. Our responsibility is to move to the center of His will. If you do not know the way, just follow His Word. It alone will lead you there. Now that is wisdom.

James 1:5 (KJV), *"If any of you lacks wisdom, let him ask of God, that giveth to all men liberally, and upbraideth not; and it shall be given him."*

Lord, we come to You humbly and ask for wisdom not only to choose You but wisdom to remain in You, anchored in Your love and care. As liberally as You grant it, joyfully we receive it. For You alone are our center, and we run to You so that we might find shelter, safety, protection, prosperity, and balance. Our desire is to not be plucked out of the hollow of Your hand by wrong choices and inordinate desires. But so that we may remain humbly submitting to Your will and committing our way and our work as an offering poured out for Your honor and glory. We only ask that You receive our sacrifice and person with joy. In Your name we pray. Amen.

PERCEPTION DEMANDS A CHOICE

Matthew 5:8 (KJV), *"Blessed are the pure in heart for they shall see God."*

What does it mean to be pure in heart? Does it mean for a man to be perfect and without sin by his own merit before God? Or does it just refer to some future assessment when this life has come to an end? Could it be some modification of the believer right before a man approaches the throne of God? The word for "pure" in Greek is *katharos*, meaning clean or pure. The psalmist David's request of the Lord in Psalm 51:10 was to create in him a clean or pure heart and to renew a right spirit within him. Here David is made aware of his undone condition through the knowledge of God. God had revealed Himself to David on many occasions and showed him His faithfulness, lovingkindness, goodness, favor, power, provision, protection, and mercy. David perceives God to be God, and now before a holy God, David is repenting and asking God for forgiveness, requesting a clean slate and that God may write His words or instructions for living upon. He wanted his slate wiped clean of a marred past from the clutter of lustful and foolish words, thoughts, and choices that have served as a distraction and stumbling block to living a righteous life.

David had been given the gift of perception. He not only saw God but was given the gift of seeing his undone state and utter unworthiness of the blessings of the Lord. He had been shown that the eyes of the Lord were on his life, and God was displeased with him in his transgression. David's heart was broken at the fact that he had brought displeasure to God, yet his heart was bent to Him. On the backside of the mountain, he tended sheep and communed with God. He became familiar with the Spirit of the Most High

THE POWER OF THE CHOICE

God. He loved God's presence, and God loved him. He called for it in worship, longed for it in prayer, rejoiced in it in praise, and repented before God when in transgression. Whatever situation he found himself in, he knew he was not alone. The presence of God was his keep, his companion, his joy, his answer, his song, his chastisement, his redemption, his victory, and his humility. There-fore, his cry, his yearning for God, is seen in his passionate request. *I know that I have done wrong; I know that I have forsaken my first love, but, God, show me Thy mercy; do not punish me in Your anger—wash me, and I will be clean and useful to Your just cause. Let Your word be my guide and mission. Do what You must, God, to bring me back in right standing with You, but don't take Your Holy Spirit from me. Create in me a clean heart. A heart cleansed from the pollution of self, Satan, and sin, and renew a right spirit within me. Holy Spirit, speak ever so softly the words that bring life and hope. Whisper direction and guidance from Your holy place into the hiding place of my heart.* His word is spirit for David to hide in his heart, study, and live by.

Before this creation of a clean or pure heart, there must be a perception given from God's truth of the degenerative and corrupted state of the heart of the one requesting His action. There has to be a revelation, a view of himself and his displacement from the will and purpose of God caused by his own choices. They come to an understanding of the validity of God's judgments and the consequences of sin. This is a perception that could only warrant a cry of repentance from the transgressor, and his only remedy is leaning wholly on the grace and mercy of a merciful God. This is the encounter where God can do His heart-refining work and purify the heart through the light of the Holy Spirit. The pure in heart are then bent toward God. Though they struggle in this world and are sometimes tripped up, sometimes caught up, and sometimes hung up. Nevertheless, they know where their help comes from, for they have seen or perceived God. He is retained in their knowledge...never forgotten. Sometimes pondered in moments of need, sometimes in moments of quietness, and sometimes their perception is delayed. But there comes a time when their perception is awakened, and they see Him. He is always drawing, speaking soft words of truth that gently tug us to the center of His will. God skillfully and carefully adjusts the lens of life until we see Him clearly as the way, the truth, and the life. This brings about the only godly peace and love that we will ever know in this life. This truth God plans for, He is patient and waits for, and with great joy, He acts on. The moment perception takes place and He is allowed entrance into our hearts to do what He alone can do and He does best...He purifies. Let us explore.

Perception is an understanding produced by revelation, a realized knowledge, and affirmation of offered information. It is what you know, the understanding drawn from a particular incentive or stimulus that is introduced to you. Perspective is your take on a particular issue. That take or point of view is based on the knowledge you have received and the circumstances and experiences you have encountered and encounter. It is the way you view the subject from where you are, your angle from the collective of your own position and previous understanding. Perspective is how you define the thing viewed, heard, or experienced. It is the angle from which you gain insight on a presented subject or issue. Perception is the product of the lens *you* look through.

Attitude is how you set your mind on what you know after the assessment and insight have been gained. It is the stance you take on a choice. It is your standpoint or the posture you take after considering a subject or issue. Your perspective, your take on what you have perceived, frames your attitude. Your attitude determines your persuasion to act: to retreat, stand still, or move forward in your understanding. Your attitude reflects the compass of your perspective and can produce negative or positive actions. But make no mistake about it—after receiving revelation or perception, a choice is demanded, and that choice will be revealed through the processes of your perspective and attitude.

Let us look at a simple example of perception, perspective, and attitude in an active scenario. Just imagine you are at a restaurant, and the waiter sets a glass of water on the table of one of its patrons. You see, the glass of water has been filled halfway. The patron sees or perceives it and recognizes that it is a drinking glass with some water in it, but it is not full. This is his perception. From that knowledge, his perspective will be instrumental in determining what attitude he has about the glass of water. His perspective is the glass of water is half empty, and that is how his view defines it. His attitude toward the glass of water is rejection, and he demands the waiter take this half-empty glass of water away and bring him a full glass.

THE POWER OF THE CHOICE

The waiter takes the glass of water from the table and proceeds to take it to the kitchen. On his way to the kitchen, there is another patron coughing violently and grasping for the waiter and the same half-filled glass of water. He, too, sees what the first patron saw, but his perspective is different.

He sees a glass of water half full. He knows that this water could save his life and, at the very least, still his discomfort. After partaking of the water, he graciously thanks the waiter for the water that has brought peace and comfort to his situation. Both men have perceived the knowledge of the stimulus or subject, the perceived glass of water filled halfway. The perspective is determined from each man's point of view. From that point of view, the choice of how to treat the subject is made, and an attitude of how to proceed is decided. The first patron opted to reject this half-empty glass of water, while the coughing patron opted to gladly receive the half-full glass of the life-saving brew. Two men, two different perspectives, and two different attitudes about the same half glass of water and the waiter that offered it. The offering to one man was an insult—to the other, a gift. But each man's perception is the same. It is the perception of an entity (the truth, the knowledge, the stimuli, the half glass of water) that demands a choice. It is perspective that influences the choices we make and shapes our attitudes and persuasions.

The Bible says that the spirit of man is the candle of the Lord. The source of fire and light from which that candle is ignited is the truth. Without truth perception is not really perception; instead, it is the illusion man has been living without Christ, and that is deception. It is only in Christ (because perception is a function of the spirit, and it is through and by your spirit being connected to the Holy Spirit) that we gain the ability to perceive, to understand, to know the truth in our hearts. It is the truth that illuminates the soul and causes it to agree with the perception your spirit acknowledges (perceives). Once truth is introduced, perception mandates a choice and leaves no room for debate. Reject or receive the truth. Allow or disallow the Spirit of the Living God to illuminate your heart and mind with the knowledge of Him, the life-giving impetus of the gospel. Being perceptive and receiving the truth is how we walk in the light of the knowledge of the Word.

THE POWER OF THE CHOICE

Ephesians 5:8–13 (AMP):

For once you were darkness, but now you are light in the Lord; walk as children of Light [live as those who are native-born to the Light] (for the fruit [the effect, the result] of the Light consists in all goodness and righteousness and truth), trying to learn [by experience] what is pleasing to the Lord [and letting your lifestyles be examples of what is most acceptable to Him—your behavior expressing gratitude to God for your salvation].
Do not participate in the worthless and unproductive deeds of darkness, but instead expose them [by exemplifying personal integrity, moral courage, and godly character].

The Word of God declares, "*In all of your getting, get an understanding, [a perception]*" (Proverbs 4:7, NKJV). What is an understanding without truth? It is a misconception, a fallacy, a delusion. Truth is essential for correct perception to be realized. When Jesus spoke to the Pharisees, Sadducees, and Jewish leaders that were contrary to Him and His teachings, He spoke in parables loaded with truth. The religious leaders of that era had a false perspective that they were keeping the law, and through their perspective of what keeping the law was, they considered themselves righteous. As Paul put it when speaking about himself (Philippians

130

3:6, ISV) concerning the righteousness, which is in the law, "*As far as righteousness in the Law is concerned, I was blameless.*" In many instances in Scripture, we see the religious leaders' perspective employing an attitude that attempts to frustrate the ministry of Jesus and exclude Him from being the Messiah. All the while judging themselves by themselves (not by the Word of God), giving themselves a false sense of security in their own perspective. That perspective celebrates their own self-righteousness. Therefore, they were unable to unpackage, discern, or grasp the truth wrapped in a parable, which revealed the truth that stood before them. The application of light was not accomplished because they were devoid of and resistant to understanding, being closed-minded to a more perfect knowledge. There was no openness for Jesus to explore and fill.

The religious leaders of that day lacked perception and could not see Jesus as the truth, the way, and the light. Their perspective remained contrary to the One who came to bring light because their hearts were evil.

An evil heart is one that is sealed off from God's message. That heart cannot receive the truth that brings life. Therefore, their heart is dead to life, dark, and has no entry point for the light of the world, the truth, the real life. Hard hearts, stony ground, unable to receive or perceive seed or light, they remained trapped by their own perspective, trusting in a dead seed, lost in the dark crevices of their own hearts.

A group of six military personnel gathers in the dorm room of one of their fellow airmen. Their intention, after a day of hard work, is to relax, maybe get high, have some good conversation, some laughs, listen to some music, and just enjoy each other's company. The conversation goes on for a while, then takes a turn while the marijuana joint is being drawn from and then passed from person to person. It seems they all have a religious back-ground. Even in this setting, they are comfortable talking about Christianity, the goodness of God, the anti-Christ, the rapture, and the great white throne judgment.

The room gets quiet for a moment after spending some time on the sobering topics. It is then that the airman hosting the gather-ing decides to move the conversation along, supposing he can end the discourse with a statement and move to a less serious subject. It is then he makes the declaration, "One day, I am going to give my life to the Lord and give all of this up." The room once again grows quiet until one of the young women in the group speaks in the most inquisitive tone and from the most unusual place. She, though being in the same place he is in, in the same position and condition, presents her inquiry. "What's stopping you now, Jack?" she asked. Those few words…reached into the young man's heart and awakened his perception. It was as if someone lit a match and flicked it into a bone-dry pile of grass. Those words set a fire in his innermost being. He had never experienced this kind of function. Life was being breathed into the things of the Lord that this young man had heard so many times before and knew in his heart. Truths that had been engrained from an early age and were not debatable were now being activated by these words, and his perception was being awakened by the demands of those truths. The young man now sees the Jesus that he had learned about when he was a child. He hears Him speak through this young woman. What is he going to do with this Jesus? What is stopping him now? Perception is demanding a choice.

The airmen looked around the room at all the faces looking back at him. Those faces are anticipating, awaiting his delayed response. They all notice that the question has, in some way, dismantled all his defenses. He answers like one that has given a deep query thought, "There is nothing stopping me now." It was as if he had an epiphany. It was as if the secrets of life had at that very moment been revealed to him, and he now knew what he had to do. He continues, "If the Lord spares my life, tomorrow I will be in church, giving my life to Christ." That is exactly what he does, and the five other people who are in that room follow him that night and are baptized and give their lives to Christ also.

Everyone who was in that room that evening had a paradigm shift. They all began to look at life with a different mindset, from a different angle. The truth, the light, the way, which was being pondered, found a place in their hearts and birthed another perspective. What these young men and women perceived changed their perspective. In turn, their attitude about living their lives for the Lord was changed in a positive way. Through ups and downs, ins and outs, the young man's confession of faith in the Lord Jesus Christ has held firm for over forty-two years and counting.

God is cultivating a tenacious attitude within His people as He interacts with them in their daily walk. Reassuring us by His presence, whether in the everyday subliminal things, like giving our next breath, to the blatantly miraculous things that no one else can take credit for but God. He is creating a people that cleaves to His Word and the commitment that was made to Him when we first believed.

Joshua and Caleb had that same tenacious attitude to believe God after leaving the bondage of Egypt and experiencing God's goodness while journeying through the wilderness. Out of all the children of Israel who had been delivered from Egyptian bondage and seen the mighty works God performed on behalf of His people, only these two young men, among the twelve spies sent out to survey the land and its inhabitants, emerged with the godly perspective. When looking at the promised land for the first time, the whole nation shrank back in fear at the prospect of battle. When God was trying to cultivate the attitude of a favored, victorious, blessed, faith-filled, and powerful people based on the perception of the Lord's power, His goodness, His faithfulness, and His sovereignty, the children of Israel responded with fear. God calls them stiff-necked and hard-hearted. God was revealing to Israel, all along the wilderness expedition, that He was their all in all, their

THE POWER OF THE CHOICE

Great I Am, God Almighty, a battle axe in the time of war, water when thirsty, food to the hungry, the supplier of all their needs. He was their El Shaddai, their All-Sufficient One. This was the perception of God and experience that Joshua and Caleb had stored in their hearts. This was what they knew of God. This was the reality of who God was to them, and far be it from them to frustrate the grace and purpose of the Almighty God by thinking about Him contrary to who they knew Him to be. Therefore, they had a different spirit, a transformed heart and mind. They knew that God was true, and they knew their God should do exploits—this was their perspective. From their perception and relationship with the truth, they could confidently say that Israel was well able to do battle and emerge victorious because the Great God Jehovah was with them, and that was because He was, in fact, their God. They could be confident in that perspective and move on God's Word in an attitude of faith.

Resting in what you know of God is of the utmost importance when faced with the challenges of life and of growth through trial. Who God is to you should be settled in your heart and mind, just as much as His Word is settled in heaven. You should go with the Word of God. "[*He is*] *the same yesterday, today, and forever*" (Hebrews 13:8, KJV). If He did it before, He will do it again. He will save; He will deliver; He will set free; He will prosper you; He will protect you; He will empower you; He will sustain you; He will give you peace; He will give you joy unspeakable and full of glory; He will heal you; He will defend you; He will come through and fulfill the word that you have settled in your heart!

"God is not a man that He should lie" (Numbers 23:19, KJV). What He has spoken, He will surely bring to pass. This should be our mantra and perception of the God we serve. His word is true; great is His faithfulness to perform His word in our lives; He never leaves us or forsakes us; His thoughts are good toward us continually, and we have an expected end. He is Alpha and Omega, the beginning and the end, omnipotent, omnipresent, omniscient, the everlasting and Eternal God, and it is Him that I will confidently trust in because my perception of who He is has been shaped by truth and my perspective has been heightened in such a way that I won't doubt what He says concerning any subject. Most assuredly I will not doubt what He says concerning me. When I was young, the saints sang simple songs that carried grand

meanings that ring true in my heart today.

There were songs that assured you of the reaches of the amazing love and efficacious blood of Christ. There were songs that encouraged you not to let the devil ride, infiltrate your thought life, be attached to, or have a place of authority to take or drive you where he wanted you to go. One song speaks to our text more clearly concerning trusting God and being steadfast without doubt. The song speaks of knowing God through interaction with Him in everyday life. Experience with God affects our spiritual attribute of faith. As my faith is built, I know that He loves me. I know that He has gotten me victory after victory. I know that He protects me and provides for me. In my heart there can be no doubt, and there is nothing the devil can throw at me to cause me to doubt God in my heart. Songs like this live on in my walk.

I trust Him with my life, and if He has filled you with His Spirit, know that He trusts you with His.

How we look at God and what He says and how we consider what He has already done in our lives form the basis of how much power we access and how much faith is utilized to receive from Him the unsearchable riches He has promised and makes available. This is how we excel in life. Without correct perception there is no proper perspective or demand to have a deeper revelation of God's power, purpose, and plan for our lives. A proper perception of God's mastery and power over all creation (and in particular our lives) and a proper perception of how much God loves us and to what extent He is invested in us and prepared to extend His hand to provide, protect, and promote His people will lead to a vibrant faith, producing a victorious, prosperous, and powerful life, where choosing Him is made easy.

Just as God attempted to form His perspective in the hearts and minds of the children of Israel prior to Christ, the perspective that He is forming in the church, in the dispensation of grace, is Christ in us, the power of God unto salvation and the living hope of glory. Perceiving Christ will present this perspective to us daily for every decision we have to make. Christ's perspective is being formed in us daily through the interaction of the Holy Ghost, the Word, and our faith. Giving ourselves to fellowship with the Holy Ghost and building our faith through the study of the Word adds to our depth of perception, refining our point of view until we are more like Him in power, purpose, and action. This prompts us to continually choose the high ground of progression toward Christ's likeness. The right perception demands that choice.

Ephesians 4:13–15 (AMP):

Until we all reach oneness in the faith and in the knowledge of the Son of God, [growing spiritually] to become a mature believer, reaching to the measure of the fullness of Christ [manifesting His spiritual completeness and exercising our spiritual gifts in unity].

So that we are no longer children [spiritually immature], tossed back and forth [like ships on a stormy sea] and carried about by every wind of [shifting] doctrine, by the cunning and trickery of [unscrupulous] men, by the deceitful scheming of people ready to do anything [for personal profit].

But speaking the truth in love [in all things—both our speech and our lives expressing His truth], let us grow up in all things into Him [following His example] who is the Head—Christ.

There is an openness that God is looking for in our lives. A place of opportunity like the one that was presented previously in the story of the group of airmen. A place where you let your guard down and allow God to reveal Himself to you. Like the moment Moses was led to and saw the burning bush, hearing the God of

Abraham, Isaac, and Jacob speak and give instructions for the deliverance of God's people and purpose for Moses' life.

Like the moment Saul was halted on the road to Damascus and rerouted to the road to righteousness by the risen Lord. The Lord knows and patiently waits for the moment to reveal Himself to those whose hearts are ready. Just like those young airmen were ready for the voice of the Lord to penetrate their softened hearts. Perhaps when they were children, they had been introduced to Christianity but failed to really latch on to the body of truths to which they were exposed. In other words, they heard the stories and believed them but could not perceive the subject as clearly as they were seeing Him at a later point in their lives. Retrospectively, they each had to look back in their lives and see God had never left them or forsook them but was always there looking out for their good. Presently, they had to recognize His presence in the room. His omniscience, longsuffering, and mercy waited for that day, that moment, to reveal the reality of His grace to the young servicemembers.

Now the God of heaven is revealing Himself in a greater way to you. Asking that you perceive Him for the great God and

THE POWER OF THE CHOICE

Savior that He is. Is this your moment of openness, where you rest in the knowledge of Him and allow Him to saturate your heart and mind? Is this the moment you say, "Yes, Lord, today is the day I give my life to You and follow where You lead me? His desire is to take you to higher heights and deeper depths in Him. Walk with Him and commune with Him so that you might know Him in the fullness of interaction, power, and purpose in your life. This is the perception that will give you the godly perspective that you can do all things through and by Christ, who strengthens you by the power of His might. This is the choice that perception demands.

LET THIS MIND BE...

Why do we resist the proper perspective...?

The human psyche has the disfunction and distinct propensity to resist the will of God. This flaw is primarily due to what we have inherited from our first parents—the longing of the flesh to dominate the spirit and be preeminent in the life of mankind. When speaking about unregenerated man (or the man that has not received a new heart or become a new creature in Christ), the Word says in Jeremiah 17:9 (KJV), "*The heart is deceitful above all things, and desperately wicked: who can know it?*" It actually uses the word "desperately," which means that man's heart frantically and continually pursues wickedness. Wickedness is described as evil or immoral, having a mental disregard for justice, righteousness, truth, honor, and virtue. Where this evil attribute presents itself, peace becomes nonexistent, and ruin is sure to follow. The direction of wickedness is away from God, and its purpose is to take all those who follow it deeper into darkness. This is the direction the flesh leads those who follow its leading. The flesh has a mind of its own, contrary to God, embracing mischief, and looks for only self-gratification without regard to the spiritual consequences that ensue. The spirit likewise has a mind of its own and pursues and respects the things of God. A sure sign of wickedness in one's life is spiritual diminishing and bondage, which is synonymous with and the result of the choice of the mind of the flesh being preferred over the spirit.

The mind of man is the battlefield upon which the war for control of man's soul is waged. The Bible says that the mind of the flesh is warring against the mind of the Spirit, and likewise, the mind of the Spirit is warring against the mind of the flesh. Each perspective mindset is warring for placement, to be in a position to act out its tendencies, its desires, its character, and its nature. All of this being its will.

Galatians 5:17 (AMP):

The sinful nature has its desire which is opposed to the Spirit, and the [desire of the] Spirit opposes the [a]sinful nature; for these [two, the sinful nature and the Spirit] are in direct opposition to each other [continually in conflict], so that you [as believers] do not [always] do what-

ever [good things] you want to do.

This is the human condition, existing in the constant flux of this conflict. But this is where God gives hope and brings peace into the life of those who believe in Him. Those whose minds are fixated on Jesus Christ and His Word and look with earnest expectation for the comfort that only the truth-filled promises of God can bring. This is the truth that brings peace, rest, and freedom from the confusion of the aforementioned human condition.

In the previous chapter, we spent considerable time discussing perception and perspective. If we considered perception and perspective combined into one collective process, its product would be a formed opinion. In Greek, the word "opinion" is *doxa*. It is translated as opinion, judgment, or estimate, whether good or bad, concerning someone. In the NT, it is always a good opinion concerning one, resulting in praise, honor, and glory. It is the root word (*doxa*) of the English word "paradox"—an opinion that is true but contradicts traditionally accepted opinion or thinking. The word "orthodox"—being of the original or traditional opinion—is also drawn from the word *doxa*. We see this word, *doxa*, in Romans 4 appearing as glory, expressing an opinion given when the

THE POWER OF THE CHOICE

Scripture speaks of Abraham's faith and the promise God made to Him of giving him a son. Abraham gave glory to God within his childless situation. In the moment of his distress, his lack, his disadvantage, his need, his crisis, and his discontent, Abraham gave glory to God by calling those things that be not as though they were. Abraham called what he lacked and longed for in his life what God called it…filled and satisfied. Abraham spoke what God spoke over his life until the physical manifestation of Isaac. The meaning of the name Isaac is laughter.

Abraham's situation of childlessness, in the world's estimation, was designed to bring Abraham sorrow or discontent. Childlessness was considered a curse. But faith in the word of the Lord brought Abraham laughter and contentment. Abraham followed the mind of God and stated God's opinion about his situation and abandoned his own. He allowed the mind of God to exist and published it with every utterance of his name, Abraham, father of many nations. In the most transparent way, the relevance of this account relates to how the mind of God works. In Abraham's life, we see the patriarch allowing the mind of God to exist and replace the wicked thinking that would only take him further away from God's will and purpose for his life. Allowing the mind of God to exist in us is what the Lord requires of us so that the promises of God will be manifested in our lives fully. What He has promised you, He wants to birth in your life. Let us explore.

Abraham is the father of the Jewish nation and the father of faith for the world. He was the key human figure that God dealt with during the dispensation of promise. It is through this man that God chose to bring the message and revelation of justification by faith to all mankind, and that faith grounded solidly in God and His promises. In that dispensation, Abraham's faith was tried on numerous occasions, building him to the point that he had total trust in God. Through the promises of God and the walk of faith, the glory (the mind, opinion, or *doxa*) of God was manifested. Let us look at the promise that God made to Abraham concerning an heir to his fortune and promise. This was of great concern to Abraham. In his discourse with God, he had expressed this request for an heir and his concern in not having a son to continue on in the destiny of the promises God had made to him. Abraham told God that if he did not have an heir, his servant Eleazer would be the beneficiary of all that God had blessed him with throughout his life. With that

THE POWER OF THE CHOICE

said, God assured Abraham that he and Sarah would have a son from his own loins. Abraham's response to the promises of God was another snapshot of the faith God was pleased with. The Bible says he believed God and was not weak in that belief even after considering his and Sarah's inabilities and disqualifications from having children, according to the functions of the body. He still maintained unwavering faith in the One who had promised.

Romans 4:19–22 (AMPC):

He did not weaken in faith when he considered the [utter] impotence of his own body, which was as good as dead because he was about a hundred years old, or [when he considered] the barrenness of Sarah's [deadened] womb. No unbelief or distrust made him waver (doubtingly question) concerning the promise of God, but he grew strong and was empowered by faith as he gave praise and glory to God
Fully satisfied and assured that God was able and mighty to keep His word and to do what He had promised. That is why his faith was credited to him as righteousness (right standing with God).

God had made this promise twenty-five years prior to

Abraham and Sarah receiving Isaac. When promised, Abraham was physically well capable of fathering a child. But God tested the resolve of Abraham's opinion by waiting until Abraham considered, judged, and estimated his body dead and the womb of Sarah incapable of sustaining a child. Still, the man of God made a conscious decision to allow God's word to settle in his mind and find permanence in his heart, to exist there. And Abraham counted the word of the Lord alive enough, powerful enough, sufficient enough, and well able to carry out what He had promised.

Our Father God does not regard time, length, or lack of it. He does not regard how much strength we have or weakness. The Lord does not regard your riches or lack thereof, your earthly alliances, or personal opinions. What God regards is your opinion about Him and His Word. His Word is His mind, and God is seeking those out who will allow the mind of God to exist in them. Those who will let His mind be and allow a spiritual reboot, becoming the new creatures that will demonstrate the will of their Savior and King. I pray that it is you who allows His thoughts to be your thoughts and His ways to be your ways, that the content of His mind, for you, exists in the chambers of your heart. A mind that agrees with His Word and steps that follow the ordered pathway, creating a life consistent with God's viewpoint and demonstrating God's will in daily living.

God's promises are presented in time and not without testing the resolve of the one who has been promised. Abraham was presented a promise that, through the test of time, became more difficult and unlikely to be accomplished if his dependence was in his own body to get it done. Over time it became an apparent and impossible assignment that he had no control over, but his faith had the attention of the One who did have control. He had to have the mind of God on the matter. It had to be done through faith in God's Word and the opinion that God is well able to accomplish whatever He says.

We, as believers, have to come to the conclusion that it is not our responsibility to bring the promises of God to fruition. It is our responsibility to rest in the truth and let His mind exist in the center of our being. In this we give glory (His opinion reigns) to God by abandoning the limited opinion of man and embracing the limitless opinion of God on what we can do or have.

It is when we operate from His mind that we can do all

things through Christ, who strengthens us, and all things are possible to those who believe. This is not only Abraham's story but our testimony to the world that our God can and will do what He has promised for those who believe and agree with the opinion that God has of Himself. He is more than *"able to do exceeding abundantly above all that we ask or think, according to the power that worketh in us"* (Ephesians 3:20, KJV). God is more than enough! What is your opinion on that truth?

As powerful as God is, it is also true that He does not operate in your life beyond the boundaries of your belief. In other words He does not force you to do His will. He will always do an opinion check to ensure that your mindset is in sync with His will. A father brought his son to be healed by Jesus. The child had an evil spirit that had been vexing him, casting him into the fire on occasions and into the water on others. To add insult to injury, the boy was mute. This situation was causing the child to pine away as his father was feeling anxious for a healing and even more helpless to better the child's condition. Through his love for his son, the father was constantly in distress by this evil spirit also, fearing for the life of his son. The distraught father's plea to Jesus' disciples was that this evil spirit be cast out, but they could not perform his request, though they tried. Upon Jesus' return, He told the child's father if he could believe that "all things are possible." Through tears, the father replied, "I believe, but help thou my unbelief." There are situations in our lives that cause us to pause and pay more attention to the problem than the Word of God. God, I need a pure heart of belief in You. I repent of my stutter, step at the Word of God, and set myself in alignment with Your declaration over my life. With great confidence, I step into the truth of Your Word, in full expectation of truth's manifestation.

Jesus just needed the mustard seed faith to perform that miracle. That faith had to be on one accord and aligned with the mind of Christ. In my mind, I can see Jesus taking that father by his face and facing him eye to eye. Jesus draws close to him so his focus is only on Jesus and the words that He is uttering. Getting into his head to realign his thinking to agree with the truth. The fasting and praying that Jesus spoke of were to diminish the mind of the flesh, give placement to the mind of the Spirit, and space for that mind to be enlarged in our soul. When we are one with the mind of Christ, miracles can happen. Oneness with Him allows the richness of the kingdom of God to be accessible to us.

Proverbs 23:7 (KJV):

"For as he thinketh in his heart, so is he."

Christ thought it not robbery to be equal with God because He shared the same opinion His Father had. He shared the same mind; therefore, He got the same results. Let this mind be in you, which was also in Christ Jesus, who thought it not robbery to be equal with God. This was the opinion of Jesus. He thought to have the same estimations, judgments, and expectations that God had, which produced the same power, majesty, exaltation, and glory that God possessed over any situation. This is reigning in life, the hope of the saints in light. Our endeavor is to have the mind of Christ that manifests the glory of the Lord throughout the earth. Through and by the gift of Christ, we are now joint heirs with Him. Having the power of God work in us and through us in its fullness is not robbery but the result of having His mind, His opinion, and His glory. It is His mind in us that supplies the preeminence and peace to live a powerful and victorious life. This is the opinion that we walk in. *"For it is God which worketh in you both to will and to do of his good pleasure"* (Philippians 2:13, KJV). Just as Mary told

THE POWER OF THE CHOICE

the servants at the wedding at Cana, "Whatever He says, whatever is in His mind for us to carry out, do it." His thoughts toward us lead to glory. His opinion is the things that are impossible for man are possible with God. Jesus is saying to you, "Whatever your circumstance, situation, need, or desire, if it is in the Word of God, you can do this." Whatever this is, Jesus says, "Let My mind be… in that situation." Allow His mind to exist in and saturate your heart and soul through and by His Word. Choose the mind of the Spirit and resist the mind of the flesh, and you will know the power of a good and gracious God in your life.

GOD OVER GIFTING

Psalm 116:12 (KJV), *"What shall I render unto the Lord for all his benefits toward me?"*

Receiving a gift from someone who admires you and you, in return, admire them is truly a beautiful thing. The gift, many times, denotes the level of devotion the giver has for the gifted. The giver and gifted alike have the opportunity, in time and through relationship, to see the fruit of the continuity of commitment reciprocated repeatedly throughout their lives. Gifting is truly a beautiful concept: the giving of something valuable to another without the expectation of receiving a gift of the same value. If we expect something of the same value, what we have is a trade, not a perfect gift. It is a true statement; the gifts that men have come from God, according to James 1:17.

James 1:17 (NIV), *"Every good and perfect gift is from above, coming down from the Father of the heavenly lights, who does not change like shifting shadows."*

The gifts the Father gives are called good and perfect gifts, and they are given out of His love for His creation. Good because they are given freely and have no evil in them, and they are perfect because they are flawless and flawlessly given out of God's gracious affection for His creation. The Bible says that the gifts and callings of God are given to us without the prerequisite of repentance. His yearning desire is to see that kind of love reciprocated back to Him voluntarily, loyally with passion, throughout our lives. Nevertheless, what you do with your gifting is your choice.

These gifts are many and varied in the lives of men. To name a few: knowledge, understanding, wisdom, expertise, diverse physical abilities, social abilities, language, life, sight, hearing, touch, taste, smell, leadership skills, oratory skills, position, power, outward physical riches, inward spiritual riches, prophecy, tongues, pastors, your ethnicity, strengths, weaknesses, youth, time, old age, and so many other gifts man has acquired from God. The Bible states that we are fearfully and wonderfully made. A masterpiece of God's design who, through the conglomerate of God's gifting, has been equipped to be a powerful entity in the world. Created to thrive and live in the experience and appreciation of the benefits we have been granted.

These gifts supplement our lives in such a way that we occasionally (as human beings do) become so dependent and enamored with them that we struggle with cherishing and preferring them over the very God that gives them. Sometimes we give our gifts preferences and a badge of privilege they truly do not deserve. This partiality and undo exaltation transforms a good and perfect gift into an idol. The idol is the idea behind a physical manifestation. It is the thought that gives an idol influence. The notion that an idol can perform some tasks or bring some blessing that only God can accomplish is foolishness. The idea that Baal or Ashtaroth could do anything that God could do was an idol and fruitless thought (no pun intended). Absolutely an idol thought that has absolutely no power. Just a bad idea only represented by a statue or inanimate object. The gifts we receive from God and offer back to God voluntarily and with joy should not be idolized but sacrificed and presented to Him like the crowns the twenty-four elders cast at the feet of Jesus. Relinquishing all authority to Him, they bow in subjection to His sovereignty and bask in the power and efficacy of His grace. There is none more important than God.

This text is to expose the erroneous place of importance

afforded to these ideas and giftings and to shed light on how we properly approach God with our gift. The gifts are important to our purpose, but our preference, in respect to these gifts, is a matter of choice and can convert these gifts into an obstacle in our relationship with God. If you have exalted a gift in your life, you can identify the thing you have idolized by recognizing that it draws you away from glorifying God, which is an idol's purpose. A gift turned idol also tempts you to get glory for yourself through and by your working and honoring it. It may be that your gift is making room for you in an area you know is not God's will for your life. You let the glory and gain of it entice you. You begin to reason with the idea of its importance and adjust your psyche for its elevated acceptance. You make excuses for it and increase room in your heart for it until you suggest with doubt that it may be what God wants. As deceitful and untrue as it is, for a season a part of you may feel the gift's offering is more rewarding and more pleasing than what God is giving in the moment. You may see the pleasure of it, the popularity of it, the gain of it for a season, but deep inside your heart...you know. It is your own way, a thought or idea that has exalted itself above the knowledge of God, an idea that should

158

be captured and cast down. It subtly lures your heart away from loving and obeying your Heavenly Father. I know that it is hard to hear, but it is an idol. That thing that arrests your devotion, draws you delicately away from His service, and eventually impacts your life more than the Lord Jesus is an idol. God is good, and the gifts that He gives are good and perfect gifts. But a gift can be distorted by the receiver's partiality to it. It is when the gift is preferred over the giver that the offense is committed. To ensure the reader understands the correct order of preference that God requires, let us reiterate.

The Giver and His Word are much greater and deserving of that place of priority in our hearts than the gifts He gives us could ever be. Forever it is God over gift.

Even after we are saved and have received the gift of the Holy Ghost, have studied the Word, begun to work in our ministry, and become acquainted with the anointings and our giftings, we must still be cognizant and vigilant of the fact that we have another enemy. We have an enemy called the flesh that we fight daily. An adversary whose aim is to distort our view of God through lust and exalt its desires and the fulfillment of them to its own glory. Adam and Eve had been given extraordinary gifts, but the tree of the knowledge of good and evil (the gift that had not been unwrapped and presented to them…yet) was the very gift that Satan used as a tool to persuade our first parents to exalt flesh rather than exalt God and His Word. Flesh itself was a gift before it was corrupted by its insatiable addiction to more and more of the knowledge of good it could not perform and evil it could not resist. Its lust drove it out of the realm of moderation into self-destruction. Flesh unchecked will lead you to sin and sin to death. It will always exalt the gift above the giver, revering supremacy of itself for the purposes of self. Flesh has one mind: self-absorption, self-exaltation, self-gratification, and finally self-destruction.

We see this same degrading process happen in Lucifer in Ezekiel 28 and Isaiah 14. Lucifer was called the anointed cherub that covereth. Lucifer himself was beautiful and gifted above measure, and he prided himself in how God had created him, exalting himself in his own mind, above the stars of heaven, making himself like the Most High.

Isaiah 14:12 (KJV), *"How art thou fallen from heaven, O Lucifer, son of the morning! how art thou cut down to the ground, which didst weaken the nations!"*

Improperly regarding His gifts and not giving glory to God for them, Lucifer exalted his beauty and talent with prejudice, jealousy, pride, and haughtiness in his own heart and mind, reaping for himself a great fall and destruction, taking a third of the heavenly host, condemned, with him. His God-given gift became an idol to exalt self, which ultimately ruined the created. My father-in-law Bishop James Straughter often said, "You can make an idol out of anything." This is a true statement. Let us explore.

Cain and Abel were the first from Adam and Eve. Both had excelled in the giftings that God had graciously given them. Yet their story has nuances of the human experience that we sometimes glaze over. Sometimes we find it hard to see ourselves in the tragic but true story of Cain and Abel. The envy, pride, jealousy, murder, and unrepentant nature revealed in this accounting makes many turn a blind eye to the parallel of Cain's existence to our own. We have been deceived by our own flesh into thinking that we are intrinsically good when the truth is quite the contrary. Men are intrinsically wicked without the intervention of God's Word and our faithfulness and obedience to it. Jeremiah says it like this:

THE POWER OF THE CHOICE

Jeremiah 17:9 (KJV), *"The heart is deceitful above all things, and desperately wicked: who can know it?"*

Let us look a little closer.

If we really want to know who we are without God, this telling story would be a good place to start looking. This story lays bare the core and true nature of man without our Savior. The transparency of it may be somewhat unsettling once we determine and settle into the fact that this is our story. This is self, parading in its unrighteous glory. It is us giving improper placement to a gift and rejecting God and His Word.

The story begins and focuses on two individuals, two brothers who have been graciously gifted by God to excel in their respective gifting. Their gifts were the collective of what God had given them to experience life. To some extent their gifts defined them. Cain had been gifted with the ability to grow things from the earth. He was a tiller of the ground. His gifting is clearly identified in the Word. His brother Abel's gift was identified as well, pointing out his ability to raise and care for sheep. The Bible says he was a keeper of sheep. Abel's gift and Cain's gift were a convenience to both brothers, not an advantage to one. Each gift was important to

162

their existence and in line with God's purpose. In other words, God had no problem with either man's gift. Both gifts were assigned by the Creator. To God the physical value of their gifts equals the importance of each man's gifting important to the gifted and certainly to those who were in their family and community. Yet there was another entity that had to be considered and satisfied, and that entity was God, the Giver of gifts.

There was a directive issued, a word given that brought honor and glory to God, an ordered sacrifice that God had required and had respect to. His instructions were simple and needed to be followed to retain His acceptance, favor, and blessing. Therefore, the directive and obedience to it were the elements that fulfilled God's good, acceptable, and perfect will.

This instruction had to be something that was passed to them from Adam or even more damning to Cain; the word came directly from God Himself. The Bible does not really clarify, but the implication is that they received the instructions, being that Abel's offering was by faith, according to Hebrews 11:4. Faith cometh by hearing and that by hearing the Word of God. One offering was considered righteous, and the other not. Righteousness

THE POWER OF THE CHOICE

denotes that there had to be a directive or a standard to follow to be considered righteous or unrighteous. A specific sacrifice had to be offered, a sacrifice that required blood to be shed. Simple enough, right? Just get a lamb, the sacrifice that God requires, and humbly sacrifice it to God. The results will be you remain in His favor and continue in your gifting, purpose, blessing, and favor.

Cain has a break in his feelings about God's directive and about this subject of sacrifice. The issue, in reality, was not sacrifice or jealousy. The issue with Cain was disobedience. His pride fueled his obstinate defiance, his refusal to obey God's Word. He inaccurately estimates his gifting of fruits and vegetables, the work of his own hand, to be just as valuable as his brother Abel's gift of a lamb. Cain's approach to God was honoring the value of his gift more than honoring the word of God, who gave the gift. This he did by not following the directive set by God. As Cain has exalted his gift and his own directive, he wants God to agree with his exaltation of it by accepting it as sufficient. This God would not do. He could not accept disobedience and call it righteousness, just as He could not accept a lie and call it the truth. God is a righteous God who cannot lie. Cain put so much value in himself and his self-effort, he was blinded to and had no regard for God's location in his heart. Cain also failed to estimate the value of the approach and process when presenting a sacrifice to God. Whether lamb or vegetables, each gift held value in the realm of men and one not greater than the other in the natural. In sacrifice to God, it is faith in His obeyed word that has value. All through the Word, we receive instruction to hear, listen to the Lord, and obey His command, which is better than sacrifice. Faith just to obey Him and show Him a humble spirit while preferring His Word over our own reasoning, our own suggestion, our own arguments, and our own opinion is what God desires of His creation. Doing it like He said because He said it brings pleasure to our God.

It is not that Cain put his vegetables where a lamb should have gone, but in his heart, he put his preference where God's Word should have taken precedence. His sacrifice should have matched, agreed with, and looked like God's Word. Cain's offering was refused because it was not offered in accordance with God's Word (in faith, by love), which is His will. Therefore, Cain's sacrifice was rejected and considered wicked because it was contrary to what God said and required. This refusal did not bring Cain to repentance but instead invoked a jealous rage, a hardened heart that culminated in the murder of his brother Abel. This was all because Cain chose not to honor God over his gift. Still, his response to God's Word was rejection. He dove deeper into self. Envy, jealousy, and wrath took hold, resulting in Cain luring his brother into a disadvantaged situation, attacking him, and murdering him. This is who we are without God and His Word: self-absorbed, envious, jealous, deceitful, angry, hateful, and murderous souls. If we do not actually commit these things, we stand by and do nothing when others who are bolder than we are do. Agreement makes us just as guilty in our own hearts. Is this transparent enough? Can we see ourselves now? Then let us go further into seeing the parallel.

One of the greatest gifts that God has given us is our ethnicity. The pluralistic nature of the world's ethnic makeup is a blessing that God has bestowed upon mankind. It is, without question, a gift. When we look over the world and the many contributions that have been made for the continuity of humanity, we must stand in awe and applaud all nations, all people. Every ethnic group has played an important role in the world's progression.

As exploring ethnicity is a gift, I would like to follow its path briefly through two ethnicities in particular: the Black and the White America.

Keeping on topic, we want to bring out how the gift is exalted and then distorted while God is presented in the back seat. I do understand that these words, taken out of context, may be offensive and hurtful to some. But please understand that these words are being publicized for the exposure of the idol and not the belittlement of the people. It is truly a work of love for God and my brother.

Most understand that being Black in America, from the time of slavery to the 1960s, made it hard to be thought of as a gift, though it was. Some may disagree, being these years seemed to be the heyday of White privilege along with the forging of Black endurance, tenacity, and ingenuity. It is a fact that Black people were victimized and discriminated against on every imaginable level with impunity to those who offended them. Blacks were minimalized, thought to be and treated less than other ethnicities, in many cases considered less than human, most commonly by White America, and in direct contrast to the treatment White America received and expected in any given situation. There was a plethora of disadvantages that went along with the categorization of being Black in the United States. Just to mention a few restrictions: patronizing the same restaurants, using the same restrooms, utilizing the same drinking fountains, attending the same schools or churches that White America attended, getting a loan, or selling property. Black people in America were put in a position to give more for less and receive less for what was obviously worth more. A Black man even suspected of looking at a White woman amorously was in danger of losing his life in the most gruesome way imaginable. All these things were publicly known. Even as they dedicated and gave their lives for the protection and continuance of this country, discrimination against their acceptance was firmly kept in place when they returned from war. Always subjugated to their White counterparts, the Blacks were denied equality in the nation they pledged their allegiance to. This denial and subjugation of Black people, in general, was being carried out by our God-fearing self-respecting White brothers, most of who agreed with that current situation. This was America's mindset, and it seemed as if they prided themselves in it. You just needed your badge to be a part of that system. You needed to have the right skin color. Their ethnicity housed the idea, and the majority agreed with the systems' workings and outcome.

All of this is a fact, no speculation. Their idea: to maintain for themselves position, power, and wealth and to exclude all others became the mantra of a supremacist movement. They would go to any length to keep things just the way they were to exalt this undeserving idol god that was no god. In the southern states, laws were instituted to extinguish the Black vote so that men with the same biased mindset would become our lawmakers. Thereby, with the exclusion or minimizing of the Black vote and diminishing any Black leadership, they would continue plunging their brother deeper into this designed darkness (leading him out to a field of disappointment, lack, injustice, imprisonment, and death).

Black people were beaten; they were hung; they were shot; they were castrated, incarcerated, denied justice, belittled, and humiliated; women raped; homes pillaged or burned; and yet they thrived, excelled; they invented, educated themselves, built wealth, fought, and became the needed element to win wars and build a nation. Fighting for a country that would continue to deny their acceptance and equality, they endured. Their strength and ability to go through those atrocities and still achieve the accomplishments the world realizes and continues to achieve is a gift. Their resolve is commendable. The darkness of our skin identifies us with the suffering and the strength to overcome that suffering. The color of our skin had become the mark of who we are and what we have excelled in being, while truth be told, that same Black ethnicity had also become, to some, an idol. Truth.

So what is the sacrifice still that God needs from a people that have suffered through so much and overcome? God has not changed in His prerequisite for a righteous approach. *"And thou shalt love the Lord thy God with all thy heart, and with all thy soul, and with all thy mind, and with all thy strength: this is the first commandment. And the second is like, namely this, Thou shalt love thy neighbour as thyself"* (Mark 12:30–31, KJV). Prefer Him first. *"Thou shalt worship the Lord thy God, and him only shalt thou serve"* (Luke 4:8, ASV). It is still repent and be baptized, every one of you in the name of Jesus, and you shall receive the gift of the Holy Ghost. The sacrifice is to humble ourselves under the mighty hand of God, and He will exalt us in due season. *"Seek ye first the kingdom of God and his righteousness and all these other things [will] be added to you"* (Matthew 6:33, KJV). Do your duty, fear God, and keep His commandments. Deny yourself and follow

Him. Our gift does not qualify or give us the right to exclude proper approach nor pursue God in our own way. In our own opinion, serving Him out of our own preference, giving regard to our taxed emotions, given our troubled past or current experiences. This idol deserves no more exaltation than the idol of privilege served by our white brothers. Our priority should be a humble dependence on every word that proceeds out of the mouth of God. Our humility, obedience, and awe of God are where all nations, peoples, tongues, and ethnicities should be one before God.

I know that this is a hard pill to swallow, but I believe it must be said. In contrast to the plight of Black America, White America has enjoyed privileges and indulgences they have guarded jealously for many years. It seems they have taken advantage of Black America's strengths, exploited their weaknesses, and created disadvantages and unfair and unbalanced scales in every societal system to worsen or stabilize their brother in his disadvantaged plight. Their unity and influence governed by their mindset have extended their privilege in all levels of society: in business, government, finance, education, and even in the churches this mindset is seen. This privilege, in many instances, has been administered preferentially because of the color of one's skin and agreement to the mindset. In the past and present, this same privilege gave liberty to some harboring this attitude to commit many physical and psychological injuries and atrocities throughout the years with immunity. Their privilege via their ethnicity is strengthened by their ability to agree and stand together in their undertaking. Through privilege more favor is granted to those of the same ethnicity, of the same mind, by which the idol has an enormous following, some passive and some aggressive but consciously agreeing. It has been proven that being White in America automatically gives you an advantage in almost any arena.

In 2016, I saw the rise of another kind of presidential candidate. Who many have considered them an insolent, vile, and unscrupulous man who, from some speculations, has been described as a malignant narcissist who pseudo-secretly embraced the White supremacist cause. Divisive rhetoric and self-centered ideologies have raised the idol of privilege, and it is all about me and those who are like me to the highest visible level that has been seen in a very long time. While stoking the worship of self with a me-first message, particular focus was placed on the position of White evangelism in America during the 2016 and 2020 election cycles. Would they hold the gospel line and preach the message of Paul—Jesus only and Him crucified—or be drawn away to lend the power of their pulpit to the preaching of politicism? Would they run to the center and keep the balance of righteousness?

It became clear that many of them had made their choice and were all in for this man who had clearly embraced self and supported theories and actions that aligned with the White supremacist cause. It was noteworthy that it did not matter what situation their candidate found himself in; his supporters would obstinately embark on explaining it away, make imbalanced parallels, or simply ignore it. Sex scandals, campaign law violations, tax evasion, extortion, bribery, insurrection, lie after lie after unbearable lie; still, many held their allegiance and never swayed, and from the point of view of most, it seemed that the allegiance of some got even stronger.

The message moved from the campaign podium to the church pulpit. The scenario made me think on the scripture Matthew 12:34 (NKJV), which reads, "*For out of the abundance of the heart [his] mouth [speaks].*" Your content will reveal the intent of the heart. What is at work here? Is God's Word the true precedent, the catalyst, or is their own preference the seated influence—the ideology being exalted above the Word of God? How can the skewed ideology of White supremacy be embraced in the same vessel that God is embraced in? How do they support a man who worships himself and harbors the mindset of hate for another race and finds it hard to hide? With every political party polarized—and it seems that the nation is fractured, divided, and closer to disrepair now than it has been in the recent past. Instead of coming together as one nation under God, choosing God, repenting, and reasoning together, division is being stirred instead of unity—in the Senate, the House of Representatives, state and local governments, Blacks and Whites, even the church is divided. It is perplexing and seems some of the fractured segments of the nation are sufficed to let the whole house fall if they do not get what they want. Selfish, devilish selfishness. They have a gift to be united in a cause, but it is clearly perverted. These have preferred their gifts over God, and with this power, even though they say, "In God we trust" with their mouth, it is the intent of their hearts to build on their own selfish lust, extending the idol of privilege. Foolish self-serving leaders, God has

174

seen and will judge. They have feigned righteousness and followed their own way. Their continued following will ultimately lead to defeat and shame for the nation.

Proverbs 14:34 (NKJV), *"Righteousness exalts a nation, but sin is a reproach to any people."*

Whether it is a unified mindset to preserve privilege or the pride in your own strength to overcome suffering and mistreatment, our gifts of ethnicity will make room for us. The question is where that room will be made. Room for us to succeed in obeying or for us to fail in rejecting what God has commanded. Blessings and cursings are not determined on how popular a gift is with the masses but on how you approach God in reference to His Word. As you present your gifting, regardless of the culmination of what God has given you in your life that defines you, we pray that you now approach the altar with the mindset of God over gifting, adhering to His desire over our own preference of approach. Offer to God what He requires. That is obedience to our Lord, which is better than sacrifice.

Precious God, we come humbly before You, acknowledging Your worth and Your greatness over and far above anyone or anything. Thank You for all the gifts that You have afforded us in this life. Through them we see the overwhelming love You have for us. Again, we thank You for the proper perspective to see that gifting and how You have purposed it. We repent and reverently cast at Your feet the crowns that You have gifted us with, and we have errantly exalted. It is our desire to love You with all our heart, mind, and strength and to love our neighbor as ourselves. We admit flesh and its deception had us captive, but the truth You have revealed to us and we walk in has made us free. We will endeavor to keep our minds forever stayed on You. You, through and by Your grace, will keep us in perfect peace. We pray that our eyes will ever be open and set on the truth of You so that we will not err in following but obey the steps ordered. To You be honor, glory, and majesty forever. Amen.

THE SUM OF ALL THINGS

Ecclesiastes 12:13 (ABPE), *"The end of the matter in its sum: listen to everything and be in awe before LORD JEHOVAH, and keep his commandments, for this is of One Craftsman which is given to every person."*

We come to the concluding chapter of this endeavor in hopes of expounding upon the concept of the sum, the conclusion or completion of the whole matter. While musing through different translations of the Bible, it is in the Aramaic Bible that our interest is piqued. It is here the word "sum" gives added enlightenment to this writer's understanding. The sum of the matter comprises the whole life of man, imaging and calculating all deeds collectively. The matter being man's life in its past, present moment, and its continuation, being the very experiences enjoyed or feared, those we flee from or run to. The matter is the conglomerate of what we choose to engage, those events in each man's life that collectively define his life until and to its conclusion. The Latin meaning of the word "sum" is "to become." You become the sum of your life experiences according to the intent of your heart. Thus, the rendering in Latin would be the end (conclusion) of the matter (life) in its sum (becoming) is to listen to everything and be in awe (reverent fear) before the Lord and keep His commandments. The matter is your life becoming what thus says the Lord. It is He that we should be in reverent awe of lest we squander what the One Craftsman has given to every person. That is the choice to become what God wants for you. The sum of the soul that chooses God and the sum of the soul that doesn't are known factors and will always remain the same. It is the matter that must be added to or taken away from to equal the sum. Let us explore.

The totality of an individual's life, in essence, should be

equal to the word we choose and experience in it. In accordance with God's Word, our choices should be governed by our respect for Him and our faith in His every decree. In the parable of the sower, the Bible says a sower went out to sow seed, and some seed fell on stony ground, and some on thorny ground, and some fell on good ground. Each place of planting represented the heart of man. Each place was different in its atmosphere, ability to house the seed, and degree of ability to produce fruitfulness. Each was different in its yield of harvest because each type of soil variated in how the seed was processed within it. The quantitative value or sum of the harvest aligns with the productivity caused by the life choices of the heart that housed the seed in each given scenario, whether it be the lack or abundance of productivity.

Only the heart that was unfettered by stony ground or weedy attributes was able to produce a harvest that answered the sower's harvest expectations.

Solomon put it like this: the end of the matter in its sum is equal to revering and respecting the Word of the Lord and keeping His commandments. The heart of the true believer needs to be devoid of the stony thoughts and word-choking, weedy thoughts

THE POWER OF THE CHOICE

that set themselves to be a permanent flesh-preferring, spirit-debilitating fixture in your life. It is time that the church breaks up that fallow, hard, uncultivated ground. It is high time that we remove the non-productive, space-stealing stones and purpose-choking weeds to expose the good ground of the heart. As the heart embraces the seed, the nutrients of faith and love will grow the seed of the Word into the image of Christ in our lives.

In our main scripture, when the writer states the words "the end of the matter," the end of the matter is the conclusion of choices made that define our experiences as godly or ungodly, righteous or unrighteous, faithful or fearful. He exclaims to make these choices in reverential fear of the Lord is the whole duty of man. It has been made abundantly clear that man is a self-determinate being, and it is our choice to obey the Word or not, and we have the distinct right to do with this precious gift of life whatsoever we want, pending a reward or punishment for our choice. This is the reason for so much perversion in the world today. Men have forsaken God and gone their own way, allowing the stones to remain and the weeds to grow wild and unchecked, producing more and more ungodliness.

There is a way that seems right to a man, but the end

thereof is destruction. We understand that there are many answers to life's dilemma, but once introduced to God's Word, which is the truth, we conclude that there is only one right answer to life's equation, and that answer is yes to the will of our Lord and Savior Jesus Christ. He alone is the answer, the sum, the conclusion, the truth, the life, and the way to become what God commands and expects. Our duty as children of God and citizens of His kingdom is to reverence and respect our Lord and heed His Word. He, therefore, is how we become what God desires and the very essence of what He was. For it is His Word that has the unique ability, through and by our obedience to it, to make our living equal to and mirror our whole duty.

This treasure of life that we have received from our birth has been somewhat of an addition problem that we add experiences to daily. It is important that we build wisely upon this life and add only those things that have righteous value and subtract those things that are contrary to that expected end. These experiences add up to the sum of all things in our lives. The sum of all things answers the question of who we will serve—good or evil, light or darkness, Spirit or self, God or Satan. The sum of your life will give definitive answers to the questions posed of faithfulness or fear, heaven or hell…life or death.

It would be fair to say that life without the knowledge of God, which exposes clarity of purpose, position, and power, is an enigma, to say the least. Without God, life is a hopeless and un-solvable problem, an unescapable pit that engulfs all men. This truth needs to be acknowledged individually by every man, wom-an, and child. This life coming to its conclusion without the Lord is an incomplete equation of sorts that can never equal its fixed sum, a question without an answer, a tragic and regrettable conclusion. Incomplete. Undone.

An equation is a statement where the values of two math-ematical expressions are equal. This is indicated by the sign =. When referring to mathematics, the sum of an addition problem is equal to the total of all addends. Example: $1 + 1 = 2$. The ex-pression on the left side of the equal sign $1 + 1$ (the addends) is equal to the expression on the right side of the equal sign 2 (the sum). Thus, the problem is solved. The sum is the conclusion of the equation. The left side of the equation is equal to the right side of the equation. The Lord is saying that to fear God and keep His commandments (left side of the equation) should be equal to the whole duty of man (the right side of the equation). Our lives should be equal to every word that proceeds out of the mouth of God, and the sum of our lives is to become just that. In Christ, our standing is we have already become equal to the word. In our state, we are continually becoming equal to the word. This is an equation that is pleasing to our Lord.

The Scriptures say that Jesus thought it *not* robbery to be equal with God and made himself of no reputation and took the form of a servant who was made in the likeness of men. He was like us in His becoming flesh. In His obedience and His being the Word in its sum, He was God (Word that became flesh). He was born as a human, lived as a human, laughed as a human, cried as a human, suffered, obeyed as a human, and died as a human. Jesus was tempted in every aspect as we are, and yet He remained obedient to His duty, even unto the death of the cross. He proved He as a human was also like God in His sum by devotion to the word of His Father to do His whole will.

Matthew 4:4 (KJV), *"Man shall not live by bread alone but by every word that proceedeth out of the mouth of God."*

THE POWER OF THE CHOICE

Perfect in the execution of it, His life equaled the Word of God. He mirrored the Father. In Jesus' statements, He declared when you saw Him, you had seen the Father. That is because God was His Word, and Jesus always did what the Father said. This is who we are! Our lives are governed by the Word, which equals oneness with God. This plainly translates to the fact that what our God possesses is ours. We are one with Him. The power that He has is ours. The eternal life that He has is ours. The joy, peace, love, fulness, and all that He is has become ours through our union with Him in Christ. We are His body in the earth because we have submitted to His lordship, and by His grace He lives in us. We are complete in Him and have the full expression of the will of God in Him, which is the sum, the conclusion of all things. We have received of Him the joint-heirship that supports the Word when it states, "*As He is, so are we in this world*" (1 John 4:17, KJV). Through faith in His finished work (the sum of what He has carried out for us), He presents us faultless before the presence of His glory with exceeding joy.

Colossians 2:10 (AMPC):

"And you are in Him, made full and having come to full-

ness of life [in Christ you too are filled with the Godhead—Father,
Son and Holy Spirit—and reach full spiritual stature]. And He is
the Head of all rule and authority [of every angelic principality
and power]."

It is believed that Solomon, the king of Israel who had
been graced with the gift of wisdom and understanding above all
his fellows, ascended the throne of his father at about the age of
twenty years old. That godly wisdom was a part of the glory that
Israel was known for. It is important to note here that the source of
that glory was God. It is also believed and important to note that
Solomon penned ecclesiastics within the last five years of his life.
Though his reign started out as pleasing to God, in time Solomon
monumentally failed God when his heart turned away from the
Lord to follow other gods. Until this point in time, it seemed he
was a man after the heart of God like his father before him, mirroring David's affection for God and following the will of God
wholeheartedly. But with fame, fortune, influence, and opportunity
come temptations and unrestricted access into lustful desires. His
is the folly that weighs heavy on a soul threading the waters of this
world. Just to entertain one youthful lust can so invigorate the flesh

THE POWER OF THE CHOICE

that it grows in its power of persuasion. That lust, the besetting sin, with permission, shipwrecks an otherwise perfect walk. This is the plight of Solomon.

Diverse nations, dignitaries, rulers, kings, ambassadors, allies, and enemies alike desired to align themselves with Israel and be connected to King Solomon, the greatest king on earth. The king that God made. Many of the daughters and most beautiful women from these foreign rulers and seekers of the favor of the king of Israel became the wives and concubines of the great and wise Solomon, king of Israel.

It was Solomon's association with the constant deference to the idol gods his foreign wives worshipped that exacted a very heavy toll on his spiritual walk with God. Again, evil communications corrupt good manners. There were some in his harem whose cultural beliefs and spiritual persuasions began to influence his heart and mind through his own lust. Solomon began to set up idols for his wives to worship, compromising the covenant made with God. Eventually, he began to follow after idol gods and abandon the word of the Only True and Wise God that had brought Israel to the apex and sustaining of its glory as a nation. For this transgression, the Word says the Lord was angry with him.

In his failure, Solomon planted a seed in Israel that would lead God's people down the dark path of idolatry. Solomon had followed the yearning of his lustful heart to his own detriment. Having it all and doing it all has now, at the end of his life, revealed its ugly self as vain folly. I can imagine him reminiscing, remembering days in the temple when the presence of the Lord was all around him, and God alone was the pleasure that brought him to the pinnacle of joy. The presence of the Lord could not be mimicked or matched by any other entity or experience. Lost in the deepness of God's love and glory while God basks in the deepness and honesty of his praise, worship, and adoration. Each fulfilling the desire of the other. Deep calling unto deep.

I can also imagine Solomon's shame at knowing the richness of the presence of the El Shaddai and trading it for the dead-eyed stillness and inability of idols to produce that joy, that life, that presence, and that power. The wayward king's life is weighed in the balance and found wanting of the sum that God required of him. Somehow Solomon loosed his grip on that defining experience of completeness. He in God and God in him. At some moment in his life, he was overcome by the abundance of what he could experience in his flesh and forgot who and whose he was.

"Remember who you are."

The young lady has just graduated high school and is now headed to college to pursue her bachelor's degree in biology. She has, for the most part, been under the wings of her parents her entire life. It is fair to say that she is excited about the new journey she is about to embark upon. Along with that excitement is a little anxiety due to the newness of it all and not knowing fully what to expect.

Her parents have watched over her through every developmental phase of her life: teaching, training, praying, nurturing, chastising, supporting, laughing, crying, and instilling God in her at every turn so that she will have the wherewithal to stand and be strong in the face of adversity. They were tasked with developing her to be an influencer for good in the world instead of being influenced by the evil in it. This they endeavored to do. They have invested all they know into their child and count it as a seed to grow beyond where they have grown, shine brighter than they have shone, and go further than they have gone. She is the first of their children to attend college, and they have given her the gift of God and now have the task of letting go to some extent. Letting go to allow God space to form the relationship with her He has, through experience, formed with them.

They know that the world is going to come after her. They know some of the perils that she will face because they have faced many of the same adversarial ploys themselves. Her father speaks to her, fighting back the tears that have puddled in his eyes, "You know what has been placed in you. Always remember who you are." She replies, "I will, Dad. I will."

Always remember who you are. Remember the moment you first received Christ. Remember the humility and the awe that overcame you at the realization of His presence, the joy and satisfaction of fullness, and the overwhelming truth that the God of heaven would receive you and consider living in you. At that moment you have walked through the eye of the needle and left everything that you were attached to outside of that encounter. It is here you are humbled and stand empty and naked before the presence of the Almighty God. It is here that we stand longing to

THE POWER OF THE CHOICE

be clothed and filled by the Lord, and He obliges with His robe of righteousness and fullness of joy. Regardless of the power, position, anointing, gifting, prestige, influence, title, or any other thing we acquire in this life, we should retain the humility and awe of that moment, that first encounter.

I can see why David would entreat the Lord to create in him a clean heart. A heart that is free from the clutter of this life, where there is just God and David. Like it was on the back side of the mountain, where David tended sheep. It was there that David encountered God in uninterrupted fellowship, unfettered praise, and captivating worship. He continued with the statement, *"And renew a right spirit within me"* (Psalm 51:10, KJV). The late, great songwriter Andre Crouch penned the words that echoed David's sentiment. After the cares of life and the lust of the flesh had taken their toll, I imagine David's repentant heart echoing sincerely—a familiar sentiment...

Take me back, take me back, dear Lord, to the pure relationship that we had on the back side of the mountain. Take me back to the joy of Your presence and the pleasure of the fullness I felt there. The moments when, faced with a problem, my first response to it was to seek Your face, where every failure was met quickly with remorse, repentance, and restoration. The moment I first believed and the moments I was emptied of myself. That was when I felt the surge of Your power, the grip of Your grace, the awe of Your majesty, and I could do all things through You, God, who strengthens me. Dear Lord, let us revisit those moments.

We should always guard and endeavor to sustain that humility as we revel in the sufficiency of His grace and not be swayed or encumbered by the abundance of gifting, the longings of flesh, the pride of self, or the pleasures of sin. Pursuing either of those choices will cause an imbalance and misstep from the righteous path that God has prepared for us. We should always keep our focus on Him and every word that proceeds from His mouth. This produces perfect peace and a workman that rightly divides the word and need not be ashamed.

Know that you are His workmanship created in Christ Jesus unto good works. The Great God and our Savior, from which all blessings flow, dwells on the inside of you. Always guard and cultivate that investment that has been so graciously given to you. Let it grow you and the work the Lord has appointed to you as large as

THE POWER OF THE CHOICE

God wills it. What God wants for you will only be accomplished through your reverence for and obedience to the Lord.

In Solomon's life, not remembering who he was caused the lack of the fear of the Lord and obedience to God. Not revisiting the humility of that first encounter allowed the distractions of his world to entrap him through his own lust. Every failure in any man's life will be due to lack of the two elements of reverence and obedience, resulting in their own lust drawing them away from God. That lacking found Solomon unable to measure up to the sum that God required of him.

That simple addition problem, so elementary that a fool could get it right, yet the wisest and richest man on the face of the earth, for years, stumbled over himself and missed the right answer. Years later, wisdom and understanding brought the conclusion, the correct answer to the query of the sum of all things to Solomon. Discernment shed light on his life and revealed the futility of the path he had chosen and gave clear direction to the path that God had ordained for peace and happiness. Through the recording of his observations, he tried to reveal and warn his sons of the greatest of errors he had made in his life journey. The concluding and correcting declaration was to fear God and keep His commandment; this is the sum of all things. This is our duty. The statement is certainly simplistic in its utterance but holds the power of life in its expression and application.

Not guarding his heart is the mistake that Solomon fell victim to. There was so much he possessed, and the world was open to him. The devil stealthily waited for the opportunity to gain a foothold in the inner sanctum of a heart that belonged to God. Through Solomon's lustful and selfish pursuits, an opening was presented. This was an extremely dangerous error that had disastrous repercussions. Though he tried to rectify his error, this blunder transferred the practice of idol worship into the hearts and minds of Solomon's sons and grandsons and, through the passing of time, into the hearts of God's people. His actions as the wisest king that had ever lived built Solomon's temple and marked the pinnacle of the greatness of Israel. His actions as a backslidden, flesh-driven man who angered the Lord through His lustful choices helped normalize idol worship in the minds of Israel and brought the judgment of God on the nation. It matters how you handle and esteem your gifting. More than that, it matters where you place the Lord in your life. God alone should be esteemed, focused on, and our giftings utilized in unselfish love for the furtherance of His kingdom. Getting this out of order gives occasion to your own lust to make the very gift God gave you an idol.

First Corinthians 12:31 (AMP):

"But earnestly desire and strive for the greater gifts [if acquiring them is going to be your goal]. And yet I will show you a still more excellent way [one of the choicest graces and the highest of them all: unselfish love]."

King Solomon had acquired so much human knowledge, and yet he did not exalt the excellency of knowledge in the scripture that heads this chapter. He had experienced a myriad of pleasures, and yet there is no mention of the importance of pleasure in his writing. Riches and influence all took back seat. From his retrospective look back at all the things he had experienced in his own life, the good, the bad, and the ugly, Solomon could only equate those things and their short-lived importance with the words folly, vanity, and vexation of spirit.

It is amazing that after having so much of the world's admiration and respect, sitting in the most powerful position on earth, having riches beyond his wildest dreams, a multitude of wives and concubines, servants that would do his every bidding, access to the realizations of the conjuring's of his imagination, the finest and most luxurious of everything the heart longs for, the adoration of God's people Israel, an army led by God, the respect of his allies, the reverent fear of his enemies, and all the pleasures of this world he could claim as his to enjoy, he yet turned from the Word of the One who favored him with it all. Solomon, having access to and possession of all these things, still did not count them as valuable enough to be included in the summation of man's duty that was presented in our lead scripture. Of all the ventures in his own life experiment, pleasure-seeking things, and experiences that bring the greatest joy and pleasure to the human condition, Solomon defined it all as folly, vanity, and vexation of spirit. Vain and useless to produce the joys of purpose nor the fulfillment of righteousness. In the equation of life, the addends that produce the sum of all things were two simple statements in Solomon's estimation. Fear God and keep His commandments. In this declaration every man is stripped to the only thing that matters. God, God's Word, man, and the choice to obey or reject what thus says the Lord. Reverence the God who created you and doing what He says in His Word is the sum of all things. It is the completion of the process that God has designed—God, His Word, you, and the choice. When we observe our own lives, even as we indulge in our aspirations to obtain our hopes and dreams, we must be mindful that it is always this duty, this priority, that is at the center of all we do and the edict that man is bound to.

Man is a creature of purpose created by God for God. We were created to willingly choose to do His will and to respect with awe-filled worship the very thought of the God who has made us. For it is His divine breath that has infused us with life, and He is the essence of the living soul we became. We are connected to God, intertwined with Him through creation, and joined with Him in divine occupation. The great investment of His Spirit placed in His man and the great responsibility of purpose woven into the fabric of our being, like the invisible power of a magnet draws metal—our God ever draws us to Him.

Psalm 100:2–3 (BSB):

"Serve the LORD with gladness; come into His presence with joyful songs. Know that the LORD is God. It is He who made us, and we are His; we are His people, and the sheep of His pasture."

We are His, but God does not just leave it at that. He desires that we prosper and be in good health even as our souls prosper. Therefore, He invests in us. He fills our accounts with gifts, favor, and blessings. He credits our accounts having high expectations of a sound return on His investment. This is the concept that fills the Scriptures. Let us explore it.

"It sounds like credit to me."

When discussing the concept of investment for this chapter, I would share some of my thoughts with my nephew DJ, and likewise, he would share his thoughts with me. After hearing where I was being led by the Lord to write, he stated, "It sounds like credit to me." He was exactly right. It was God crediting man an abundance of gifts as a first sowing of love, a seeding for life's project. God's sowing denotes and expects a harvest. For His loving-kindness and graciousness to us, it should be our responsibility, duty, and fervent desire to love Him in return with our life and service. We should work the investment with a willing heart and a joyful and loving spirit. We should give Him back what He gave and with the expected increase or interest. In reverence for Him, His instruction should be heeded, our work should be accomplished, and God's return on His investment should be presented in the same constraints of love that He gave it. God has filled our life accounts with credit so that we should go into the world and profit Him by bringing glory to His name, adding to His kingdom, and spreading the seed of His Word. Thus, saving men from the darkness that awaits those that reject Him. A time when all accounts will be settled.

This is the reason we are steadfast and immovable, always abounding in the work of the Lord. The reason we preach, teach, witness, serve, write, sing, encourage, exhort, expound, go, rise, and do in season and out of season. We know who we are; we are vessels, and we reverence the God that has counted us worthy to pour His life into. We pray our lives reflect His passion and His purpose only. For it is and should be the focus of our existence to do the sum of the duty that we have been assigned. Or not, and receive the failing mark of disapproval from an unfailing God. You can receive the full blessing God has in store for those who love, believe, and obey Him. Or you can receive the wrath of a just God for rejection of His loving-kindness toward us. This is the power of the choice, and the choice is yours. As for me and my house, we will serve the Lord.

BIBLIOGRAPHY

Haslanger, Sally. "The Greek Concept of Virtue." Last modified March 16, 2017. https://virtueethicsinfocentre.blogspot.com/2017/03/the-greek-concept-of-virtue.html.

ABOUT THE AUTHOR

Humbled to be chosen, Dennis Jackson has been in ministry for over thirty years and has been a student of the Word of God for over forty years. His experiences with God, the calling on his life, and the God-given understanding of the elements of the choices he has made throughout his life have qualified him to write extensively on the power the choice holds. Dennis believes God is active in the lives of every believer to the extent the believer allows and chooses Him to be. He also believes God is sovereign and allows man the choice to serve Him…or not. He is persuaded that your choice holds the power to your eternal future and present state of being. Dennis has lived in Atlanta, Georgia, for the last twenty years and presently resides there with his wife, Genoa, his three daughters, and two grandchildren. He believes the ministry he has been assigned is to bring revelation and illumination to those who have an ear to hear and clarity to those who indulge his gift of writing and speaking. His pure aim is to bring glory to God and the gift of God's Word with understanding to the world.

Printed in the USA
CPSIA information can be obtained
at www.ICGtesting.com
LVHW011113310723
753624LV00016B/542